COMPUTERIZED BUSINESS STATISTICS

Third Edition

Owen P. Hall, Jr.
Pepperdine University

Burr Ridge, Illinois
Boston, Massachusetts
Sydney, Australia

IBM and IBM PC are registered trademarks of International Business Machines Corporation.

Printed in the United States of America.

ISBN 0-256-11755-1 (3.5″ version)

2 3 4 5 6 7 8 9 0 EB 0 9 8 7 6 5 4

PREFACE

COMPUTERIZED BUSINESS STATISTICS

third edition

Owen P. Hall Jr.

Richard D. Irwin, Inc.
Copyright (c) 1993
all rights reserved

OPTIONS: C = Configuration Menu, M = Main Menu, N = Next Page

OVERVIEW

The growing demand for increased productivity throughout both business and government has brought about a growing interest in statistical analysis. These developments, in turn, have prompted an increased focus on statistics in many business and engineering schools. The primary purpose of this courseware package is to provide the student with the capability to solve a wide range of statistically based problems quickly and accurately. The author believes that substituting computer modeling for traditional hand calculation methods increases the amount of time available for problem formulation and allows for a more in depth analysis of the results.

COMPUTERIZED BUSINESS STATISTICS (CBS)

CBS consists of this instructional text, a courseware package and a data base. The text provides a general overview on the operation of the courseware. The courseware package contains fourteen of the most frequently used statistical topics covered in todays leading schools of business. The user friendly menu driven package has been designed to minimize the need for specialized computer training. In fact, most users can be operating CBS within a few minutes.

Each of the technical chapters included in this text contain a brief program description, a technical overview of the basic statistical principle, the data input requirements, the standard model output and several demonstration exercises. The first exercise presented in each chapter has been incorporated as an example problem in the courseware.

Additionally, the technical modules contain a brief review of the basic principles associated with the specific statistical technique. This review capability helps the user develop a better understanding of the application potential and limitations of each statistical model.

ACKNOWLEDGEMENTS

Creating courseware materials is a long and involved process. We would like to thank those who have taken their time and effort to help prepare the first, second and third editions of this book. These reviewers offered knowledgeable comments and suggestions toward making a better product for instructors and students.

Amir Aczel (Bentley College)
Randy Anderson (California State University, Fresno)
Charles Branyan (Memphis State University)
Anthony A. Casey (University of Dayton)
Gilbert Coleman (University of Nevada, Reno)
Les Dlabay (Lake Forest College)
Satyendra Dutt (Delaware State College)
David L. Eldredge (Murray State University)
Stewart Fliege (Pepperdine University).
Edna Frye (Governors State University)
Edward Y. George (University of Texas, El Paso)
Stephen Grubaugh (Bentley College)
Wendel Hewett (University of Texas, Tyler)
Peter Hoefer (Pace University)
Geoffrey B. Holmewood (Hudson Valley Community College)
J. Marcus Jobe (Miami University, Ohio)
David D. Krueger (St. Cloud State University)
Stan Malik (Governors State University)
Clifton Miller (University of Texas of the Permian Basin)
George Miller (North Seattle Community College)
Lou Mottola (University of Bridgeport)
Peter Rob (Tennessee State University)
Donald L. Schmidt (American Graduate School of International Business)
John C. Shannon (Suffolk University)
Susan A. Simmons (Sam Houston State University)
Rex Snider (Troy State University)
George Vlahos (University of Dayton)
Edward J. Willies (Tidewater Community College)
Robert S. Wu (Longwood College)
Jack Yurkiewicz (Pace University)

We would like to especially acknowledge Ms. Lynda Wittstone, without whose assistance this project would not have been possible.

CHANGES TO THE SECOND EDITION

This text and the accompanying courseware package have been significantly updated as a result of user feedback over the past several years. The following new features have been added:

- ◊ Statistical Quality Control
  - Control Charts
  - Acceptance Sampling
- ◊ Block Design for Two Factor ANOVA
- ◊ Pairwise Test for Analysis of Variance (Tukey)
- ◊ Enhanced Central Limit Demonstration
- ◊ Nonparametric Runs Test
- ◊ Cluster and Stratified Sampling
- ◊ External Data File Input

TABLE OF CONTENTS

1.0 INTRODUCTION

COMPUTERIZED BUSINESS STATISTICS (CBS) is a collection of fourteen mathematical models which have been designed to facilitate a wide range of statistical analyses. The CBS package also contains a data management module for creating and editing data files.

Presented below is a list of the options available (similar to the Main Menu) on the CBS diskette:

◊ Data Base Management

◊ Descriptive Statistics

◊ Probability Theory

◊ Probability Functions

◊ Survey Design

◊ Random Sampling and Estimation

◊ Hypothesis Testing

◊ Simple Correlation and Regression

◊ Multiple Regression Analysis

◊ Time Series and Forecasting

◊ Chi-Square Analysis

◊ Analysis of Variance

◊ Nonparametric Methods

◊ Decision Analysis

◊ Statistical Quality Control

This text has been organized into chapters that correspond to the Main Menu selections. The chapters that involve statistical models are organized as follows:

Description:	A brief description of the statistical model.
Overview:	A summary description of the type of problem that can be solved with the model.
Data Input:	A concise summation of the data or data transformation required to use the model.
Model Output:	A brief explanation of the results.
Demonstration Exercises:	Several demonstration exercises that represent typical uses of the statistical tools, with brief descriptions of the output.

1.1 EQUIPMENT

The minimum system configuration requires an IBM PC (or true compatible) with 640K memory and one double-sided disk drive, plus a copy of DOS 3.1. A second disk drive, a printer, and a color monitor are optional. Graphic displays use the special text characters so a graphics card is not needed.

A separate diskette is required to store files generated by the data disk operations and MUST be PRE-FORMATTED or PRE-INITIALIZED. Note that the DOS will store a maximum of approximately 120 files on a directory. IBM users who wish to store more files on a diskette will have to use tree-structured directories.

You should also note that when your data disk is full, the screen listing of files will sometimes show only 84 file names. (This happens because the program overwrites those at the bottom.) You will then need to either exit to DOS and use the run a "directory", or use the Data Base program (#2) and the "catalog" program as described in chapter 2.

1.2 KEYBOARD

The keyboard is your method of communicating with CBS. The programs will display messages informing you of the input that is expected whenever interaction with the computer is required.

To operate CBS: simply type in numbers or letters appropriate to your current activity and then press the <enter> or <return> key. CBS will expect you to press the <enter> or <return> key after you type any complete response (i.e. a number from a menu, a file name, a number for a data value). Forgetting to press <enter> is a common source of frustration for many new users. If you do not press <enter> after you are done typing in a response, the computer will sit and wait, and wait...

On the "standard" IBM keyboard, the <enter> key has the following symbol: ◄─┘ Some IBM compatible keyboards have a <return> key to the right of the alphanumeric keys and an <enter> key to the right of the numeric keypad; both of which act as <enter>. Generally, IBM terminology will be used throughout this text to describe the keyboard functions.

Typing mistakes can usually be easily corrected by pressing the left arrow key and retyping the offending character(s). Do not enter a comma as part of a number. Commas are special characters to the computer. If you do enter a comma, the value entered will be equal to the digits to the left of the comma (i.e. entry of 12,500 would equal the value 12).

The keyboard is designed to be sensitive to a light touch and has auto-repeat; which means that it will repeatedly generate a character if you press it long enough (or too hard). The editing keys are the left, right, up, and down arrows, [home], [end], [pg up], [pg dn], [insert], and [delete] keys on the numeric keypad, and the [backspace] key. The "standard" IBM keyboard uses the same keys for a cursor pad and a 10 key pad. The [num lock] key controls these keys. *You may wish to set the [num lock] key to enable the cursor pad, and use the row of numbers on top of the letter keys.*

1.3 PRINTER

CBS supports a standard parallel printer, and uses the device label LPT1. Other printer configurations can be used with CBS if the output normally sent to LPT1 is redirected for the specific configuration. To use a printer other than the one connected to LPT1 you will need to execute several commands after booting DOS, and before starting CBS. These commands may be entered from the keyboard or executed from an autoexec.bat file. The MODE file (from the DOS system diskette) must be present to perform these commands.

If the printer is a standard parallel printer, but is hooked up to port two, simply enter MODE LPT1:=LPT2 (and press the enter key) to redirect the output. Redirection of output for serial printers is more complex, simply because there are more options and there is no true standard for interfacing. Several parameters may need to be set (i.e. parity, databits, stopbits) in addition to the baud rate. The baud rate is the only required parameter, and the baud rates available are 110, 150, 300, 600, 1200, 2400, 4800 or 9600. The defaults for the optional parameters are parity=even, databits=7, stopbits=either 2 if baud is 110, or 1 if baud is not 110. Refer to the printer manual and the DOS's MODE command (option 3) for more information on asynchronous communication.

Assuming that the serial printer is hooked up to communication port one, the baud rate is 1200, and the default parameters are acceptable, execute the following:

MODE COM1:1200,,,,P ◄┘

MODE LPT1:=COM1 ◄┘

For any printer, if printing is attempted and the printer is not hooked up, you will get a message asking you if you want to proceed. If the printer is hooked up and turned on, but is not 'on-line', the computer will stop and wait (and wait...) for you to push the printer's on-line button.

1.4 DISKETTE HANDLING

The CBS program disk is actually a very fragile electromagnetic film "record", protected by a plastic sleeve. Due to the highly sensitive nature of the black inner disk, it should never be tampered with. Avoid any disk contact with water, high heat, direct sunlight, or a magnetic field (such as a stereo speaker, a TV, or even a radio). Electric motors also generate magnetic fields. Do not bend your disks or store them in an overly dirty or dusty environment (such as the bottom of your lunch box or bookbag). A plastic storage box is recommended for all of your computer diskettes.

The disk drive has a red light which is on while the drive is in use. NEVER, NEVER, NEVER remove or insert a diskette while the 'in use' light is on. This will surely destroy the information on the diskette and may ruin the drive.

1.5 GETTING STARTED

Below is the sequence of events needed for using CBS directly from a disk drive (as opposed to having the program loaded onto the hard drive).

1. Boot Computer (insert DOS 3.1 System Diskette in 'A' drive, close drive door, turn power

   on). After booting DOS, you may remove the disk.

2. Re-direct printer output, if necessary (see section 1.3 Printer).

3. Insert the CBS program diskette in 'A' drive.

4. Insert a data diskette in the 'B' drive (if 2 drives are available)

5. Type A: to set the default directory to the 'A' drive or the program disk drive.

6. Type the 3 characters: CBS and press the enter key.

7. See section 1.6 to configure the program to "read" and "write" to the correct disks.

IBM users with two disk drives may find it convenient to use a system disk for their data disk. This is accomplished by simply formatting the data disk with the /S option (see your DOS manual), and then using this disk to boot the system as well as to store data upon.

If your system has two disk drives, You may set up a turnkey system to start CBS automatically. This is accomplished by using the EDLIN editor to create an autoexec.bat file. An autoexec.bat file is particularly convenient if you need to configure a printer before you start CBS.

The following section outlines the steps for creating an autoexec.bat file, assuming the two drives are labeled A and B. To minimize swapping, the file assumes the CBS program disk is in drive B and the data disk is in drive A. The file prompts for the date and the time, then starts up CBS. Additional commands can be added to redirect printer output and/or set the default directory on the data disk to a subdirectory. Commands can also be added to read the date and time from a clock card, set up a print buffer and/or a ram disk, load memory resident programs such as SideKick or NicePrint.

Step 1: Boot the computer with the DOS system diskette in drive A. The EDLIN file must be available to create an autoexec.bat file, so if your normal boot diskette is not a complete copy of the original DOS system diskette, put a copy of the original DOS system diskette in drive A.

Step 2: Prepare a diskette to serve as the new boot diskette. To do this:
1) Insert a blank diskette into drive B and close drive door
2) Type FORMAT B:/S/V and press the enter key.
Follow the system prompts until the formatting process is finished. The /V parameter specifies a volume label, so enter something like CBS BOOT when prompted for label.

Step 3: Set a path to EDLIN and change drives so DOS can find EDLIN, and so the new autoexec.bat file doesn't overwrite an existing file.
1) Type PATH=A:\ and press the enter key.
2) Type B: and press the enter key.

Step 4: Start EDLIN: type EDLIN AUTOEXEC.BAT and press the enter key. The computer should respond with two words: **new file**, and change the prompt to an asterisk (*). If you get the * prompt but it doesn't say new file, type a Q <enter>, then type a Y, and restart this process.

Step 5: Now that EDLIN has been started, enter the contents of the new autoexec.bat file by typing the following. (See the sections in the DOS book on EDLIN and Batch files for further information)

1. I <enter>

2. PROMPT PG <enter>

3. CLS <enter>

4. DATE <enter>

5. TIME <enter>

   ** Insert commands for redirecting printer output here **

6. PAUSE INSERT CBS PROGRAM DISK IN DRIVE B <enter>

7. B: <enter>

8. CBS <enter>

9. Hold down Control key and tap C, then E<enter>

Step 6: If redirecting printer output etc., copy any files needed (i.e. MODE.COM) to the new boot diskette. Remove new boot diskette from drive B and label it.

Your turnkey disk is now ready for use. If you wish to start CBS now, put the new diskette in drive A, and either reboot computer or type autoexec <enter>.

1.6 CONFIGURATION

The Configuration menu allows you to select the number of disk drives, the program disk drive, and the data disk drive. This menu also allows you to set the program for color or black & white video output. Throughout this manual references will be made to a *program* disk and a *data* disk.

> *Program Disk* - the diskette upon which the computer language needed to execute and run the model procedures which you will be using. Given the limited amount of space available on each floppy disk, you should not try to save your data on this diskette.

> *Data Disk* - the diskette upon which you will save your input and output files. This is the disk that will contain the actual information (data) that you want to process.

For speed and simplicity, loading CBS onto your hard drive (C drive) is the recommended course of action. If that has been done, the actual program disk will not be needed, and you should select C as your Program Disk Drive. If you have not loaded the program onto your hard drive, then you will need to insert the program disk into one of your floppy disk drives. If you only have one floppy drive, then you will have to do a lot of switching from your data disk to your program disk. Generally, your floppy disk drive will have been labeled the A drive, if this is the case you will then insert a formatted diskette into the floppy disk drive -- this will be your data disk, and you will type an A at the Data Disk Drive prompt.

1.7 MODEL SELECTION

A specific statistical model can be selected by simply moving the highlight bar to the model of interest listed on the main menu and pressing return. After selecting a model, the red 'in-use' light will appear on the drive containing the program diskette while the selected program is loaded into memory. At that point, the Program Options Menu will appear on the screen.

1.8 OPTIONS MENU

Each of the thirteen statistical modules contain a Main Program Options Menu. This menu is nearly identical for every module. There are a few exceptions where certain selections are not applicable and these are noted at the end of this section. Each model option is numbered. To execute a selection, either move the highlight bar to the desired selection or type the specific number and press the enter key. Note that any option requiring data (such as view, edit or run current problem) will respond with the message 'ENTER DATA ' if you have not entered data. Figure 1 presents the Main Program Options Menu screen display.

```
+-------------------------------------------------------+
|             Computerized Business Statistics          |
|         Statistical Module - Program Options Menu      |
|   +-----------------------------------------------+   |
|   |   0.      CBS Configuration                   |   |
|   |   1.      Enter Problem from Keyboard         |   |
|   |   2.      Enter Problem from Data Disk        |   |
|   |   3.      Enter Example Problem               |   |
|   |   4.      View Current Problem                |   |
|   |   5.      Edit Current Problem                |   |
|   |   6.      Quick Reviews                       |   |
|   |   7.      Run Problem                         |   |
|   |   8.      Exit to Main Menu                   |   |
|   |   9.      Exit to Operating System            |   |
|   +-----------------------------------------------+   |
|                                                       |
|        press  ◄─┘  to select option under hi-lite bar |
|    press number or up/down arrow keys to move hi-lite bar |
|                                                       |
|   A BRIEF MESSAGE ABOUT THE PROCEDURE ABOUT TO BE EXECUTED |
+-------------------------------------------------------+
```

Figure 1

0. CBS Configuration: This selection allows you to specify the computer's drive and monitor configuration. (see section 1.6)

1. Enter Problem from Keyboard: CBS prompts you through the steps for entering the data values for a new problem. Data currently stored in memory will be erased. The entered data can be saved on a data diskette.

2. Enter Problem from Data Disk: CBS guides you through the steps for loading a data file from your data diskette. Data currently stored in memory will be erased. **NOTE: output files can not be used to enter problems.**

3. Enter Example Problem: An example problem will be loaded into memory. This problem is generally the first demonstration exercise in the chapter for the specific model. Data currently stored in memory will be erased.

4. View Current Problem: This option displays the definition, input statistics, and data values for the problem. An output options menu provides selections for screen viewing or printing.

6

5. Edit Current Problem: An editing options menu provides selections for changing the individual data values, the column labels, and the model sub-options. The data structure cannot be modified. Editing is either fully prompted and/or follows the structure of the Data Base Management Program (see chapter 2). An edited file can be saved.

6. Quick Reviews: This option summarizes of the important aspects of the statistical model.

7. Run Current Problem: This option solves the problem currently residing in memory. An output menu contains options for viewing the solution on the screen, sending the solution to the printer, or storing the solution on an output text file. The output from the run includes the problem definition, the data values and the resultant calculations.

8. Exit to Main Menu: The program returns to the main menu. Data currently stored in memory will be erased.

9. Exit to Operating System: The program exits to your operating system (DOS) Data currently stored in memory will be erased.

1.9 OUTPUT OPTIONS

The user can choose from the following output options:

1. **Screen:** output is displayed only on the console (CRT).
2. **Printer:** output is sent to a standard line printer.
3. **Disk:** output is saved on data diskette (standard ASCII format).

A separate pre-formatted data disk is required to store the output disk file. An output file may be viewed via the VIEW option in the DBAS module or via a word processors which accepts standard ASCII files.

2.0 DATA BASE MANAGEMENT

2.1 PROGRAM DESCRIPTION

CBS has the capability to create, view, transform, edit and save data files for use with one or more of the statistical programs. A pre-formatted (or pre-initialized) data disk is needed to save data on a diskette. This program is a collection of tools for creating and manipulating data files.

** DO NOT STORE DATA ON THE PROGRAM DISKETTE **

2.1.1 DATA FILE OVERVIEW

Data files can be thought of as orderly stacks of paper. Each stack of paper is organized in a specific manner, and has a name to identify it and separate it from the other stacks. These stacks of paper are called files because you retrieve and store them in a manner similar to opening and closing a paper file in a filing cabinet.

Each time you create a file you are assembling a group of data points in a manner which you have specified. This data can now be accessed in the various formats necessary to be effectively analyzed by the models available to you in CBS.

Data files have four distinct characteristics:

1. Name: You must give each file a unique name. It is recommended that file names be related to the specific problem. The file name can be 1-10 characters in length. A two-character prefix (I- or O-) will be added to the data file name. The purpose of this prefix is to distinguish between input (I-) data files, and output (O-) text files.

2. Size: Each data file is structured in a matrix format with columns representing the variables, and rows the data points. A file may have from 1 to 10 variables(columns) and 1 to 200 data points(rows) for any variable.

The basic format for a data file is as follows:

                    Variable #1   ......   Variable #M
Row #1
: : :
: : :
Row #N

3. Variable Names: You are given the option of labeling each variable(column) with any 0-5 character name.

4. Data Values: The values of the data points (numbers inside the boxes) are the last (and most important) component of the data file. While the values of the data points can be of any magnitude, it is recommended that you avoid a data set where all the numbers are in the millions or billions. If this is the case, you may wish to go through and divide all numbers by 1000, or some appropriate number.

For a <u>two</u> disk drive system, the data diskette should be placed in the second disk drive during the start-up procedure. For a <u>one</u> disk drive system, the CBS program diskette and the separate data diskette will need to be switched before and after each data disk operation. CBS will prompt you for these diskette changes. Do not change diskettes unless you are prompted.

2.2 OVERVIEW

The CBS Database Management Model (DBAS) Options Menu offers the following selections:

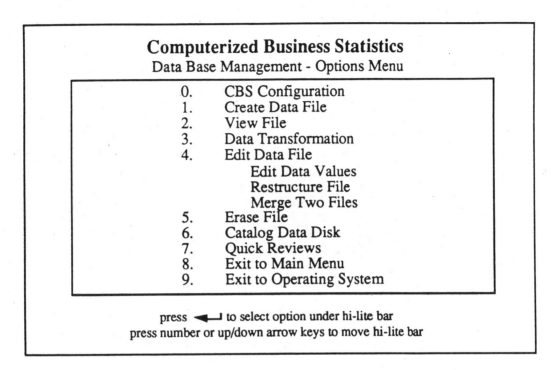

2.2.0 CBS CONFIGURATION

This menu allows you to select the number of disk drives, the program disk drive, and the data disk drive. This menu also allows you to set the program for color or black & white video output. (see section 1.6).

2.2.1 CREATING A DATA FILE

The following prompts will guide you through the process of creating a new data file:

◊ Number of Variables (Columns) in Data File*

◊ Number of Data Points:
> Number of Data Points for Variable (Column) #1
> . . .
> Number of Data Points for Variable (Column) #M

◊ Variable Names:
> Name for Variable (Column) #1
> . . .
> Name for Variable (Column) #M

> NOTE: Once you are "in the spreadsheet," you can end the data entry process at any time by pushing the "END" key. If you have not entered numbers for any cells, CBS will save the zeros, or if you are editing a file, whatever number is currently in the remaining cells. This is also true of the data entry portions of the other CBS statistics programs.

◊ Variable Values:
> Numerical Value of Data Point in Row #1, Column #1
> . . .
> Numerical Value of Data Point in Row #N, Column #1
> . . .
> Numerical Value of Data Point in Row #1, Column #M
> . . .
> Numerical Value of Data Point in Row #N, Column #M

◊ Name of Data File

* In creating a data input file outside of CBS you will need to add an additional data value at the beginning of the data file. This value corresponds to the number of variable groups. <u>Usually</u>, the value is **one (1)**. The exception involves a two-way analysis of variance data set where the first entry represents the number of row groups (2-5) and the second entry represents the product of the number of row groups and the number of column groups.

2.2.1a EXAMPLE PROBLEM #1 (Descriptive Statistics)

FILE NAME:...DS-EX

NUMBER OF VARIABLES: 1

NUMBER OF DATA POINTS: 8

VARIABLE   NAME:..X1

DATA VALUES: .... Enter data values for X1

$$
\begin{array}{l}
29.7 \\
31.1 \\
34.7 \\
38.9 \\
44.8 \\
47.9 \\
50.2 \\
56.8
\end{array}
$$

2.2.1b EXAMPLE PROBLEM #2 (Multiple Regression Analysis)

FILE NAME:...MR-EX

NUMBER OF VARIABLES: 4

NUMBER OF DATA POINTS: ....

VAR 1	7
VAR 2	7
VAR 3	7
VAR 4	7

VARIABLE NAMES:...

VAR 1	X1
VAR 2	X2
VAR 3	X3
VAR 4	X4

DATA VALUES: .... Enter data values for each variable

X 1	X 2	X 3	X 4
2.1	0	102	47
2.5	0	107	35
2.9	1	100	51
3.1	0	99	42
2.8	1	108	38
2.9	0	103	44
3.0	1	104	46

11

2.2.1c EXAMPLE PROBLEM #3 (Nonparametric Methods)

FILE NAME:..NP-EX

NUMBER OF VARIABLES:...................................2

NUMBER OF DATA POINTS:..........................VAR 1.....10
VAR 2.....12

VARIABLE NAMES:.......................................VAR 1.....POP A
VAR 2.....POP B

DATA VALUES:....................................Enter values for POP A and POP B.

POP A	POP B
20	12
25	11
15	15
19	19
30	8
28	10
27	12
21	9
22	16
18	9
	5
	8

2.2.2 VIEWING A DATA FILE

The following prompts will guide you through the process of viewing a file:

1. Specify whether you wish to view an input file (data values only) or an output file (problem data plus results).

2. Enter the name of the file.

3. Select an option from the output menu. You may either view the data on the display screen or you may send a copy to the printer. The output menu has the following three selections:

   S = Screen

   P = Printer

   R = Return to Program Menu

Enter the appropriate letter and press the enter key. If you are using a printer, be sure it is plugged in, turned on, and 'on-line'. Output for data files containing more than five variables is presented in two sections. Section #1 will contain all values for variables 1-5, and Section #2 will contain all values for variables 6-10.

2.2.3 TRANSFORMING A DATA FILE

Transforming a file or a variable consists of altering the data using one or more analytical procedures. The following prompts will guide you through the processes of transforming a data file:

** NOTE that the original data file is <u>not</u> retained in memory after performing data transformation **

1. Specify the transformation of a current file in memory, or to load a stored file.

2. Enter the name of the file.

3. Specify the column number of the variable to be transformed.

4. Select from one of the following transformation options:
M - Move (lag or lead)	**R** - Nth Root
P - Nth Power	**L** - Logarithm

The first option allows the user to *move* the data values for a selected column up or down by a specified amount. This option is useful when analyzing the impact of lag or lead variables. The resultant zero values can be removed using the edit option.

The second option takes the *nth root* of the current variable values where n is specified by the user. For example, if you wish to take the square root of the current values for a given variable you would select option #1 and then input a two when prompted. In the case of negative values, the transformation takes the nth root of the absolute value which is then multiplied by negative one.

The third option raises the current variable values to the *nth power* where n is specified by the user. For example, if you wish to cube the current values for a given variable you would select option #2 and then input a three when prompted. In the event the resultant transformed numbers exceed the largest available number, you will be given the option of either scaling the original values or terminating the process.

13

The fourth option takes the *logarithm* (base 10) of the current variable values. The logarithm of a variable value of zero will be assigned the value -1.703E-38 (the smallest available number). In the case of negative values, you will be given the option of either scaling the original values or terminating the process.

Each variable in the data file can be transformed using the above procedure. The transformed variables can then be saved in a file for subsequent analysis. This option also provides <u>scatter plots</u> for up to three variables. The user must specified which variable is to be plotted on the X-axis and which variable(s) are to be plotted on the Y-axis. This option can be terminated by pressing the "END" key. Below is example of this procedure using an existing data file.

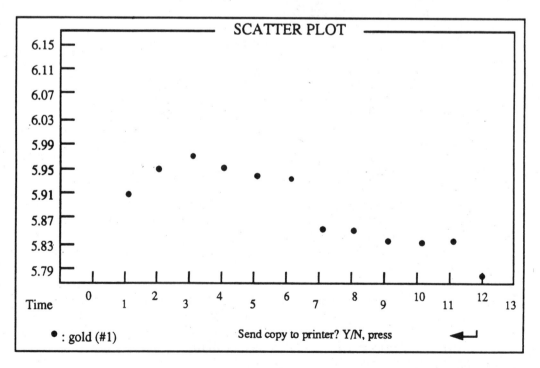

2.2.4 EDITING A DATA FILE

DBAS's Edit Menu will be displayed with the following four options:

1. Edit Data: Edits the numerical data values and/or the alphanumeric variable(column) labels.

2. Restructure File: Adds or deletes variables(columns), or changes the number of data points in a variable(column).

3. Merge Files: Merges two data files side-by-side or above-below each other.

4. Quit Edit: Returns to the DBAS Main Menu

The first step in the editing process is to select the desired data file. If a file already resides in memory, DBAS will ask you if you wish to use the current data. If you wish to use a different file, or if there is no data in memory, DBAS will prompt you for the name of the file to edit. When DBAS asks which file to edit, enter the name you gave the data file when you created it (then press the enter key). The four menu options are described in greater detail for you below.

EDIT DATA - The three selections available in the Edit Data screen are:

1. Change Data Values: Edits numerical data using a spreadsheet like format.

2. Change Variable Names: Lets you edit the variable/column labels.

3. Return to DBAS Menu

To input, change, or view any portion of the data that is not currently on the screen simply press the arrow key that points in the direction you want to move the display until the information you desire moves onto the screen. Moving the display back and forth or up and down is called scrolling. For convenience, the enter key behaves like a down arrow key when you are simply moving the cursor around the table.

To change any numerical value in the matrix simply position the cursor to the beginning of the space allocated for that data point and type the appropriate numeric characters. The cursor can be moved around the input/editing table using the quick movement commands. If you try to use one of the editing commands (i.e. "page up" or "home") and the computer does not respond, you probably have one of two problems: the num lock key is set wrong, or you never pressed enter to finish the last number entered.

15

RESTRUCTURE FILE - The restructuring commands are 'A' (to add a column), 'D' (to delete a column), 'L' (to enter a new length for a column), and 'F' (to signal that you are finished). Attempting to create a data base with less than one or more than ten variables (columns) will result in a re-prompt for another restructure command.

MERGE FILES - You will be prompted for the name of the 2nd file once the 1st file is read into memory. There can be a total of 10 variables (columns), and 125 data points (rows). Excess data points or variables will be dropped from the 2nd file.

EXIT EDIT - Returns you to the DBAS Main Menu (not to the operating system).

2.2.5 ERASING A FILE

Erasing a file from the data diskette deletes the entire file rendering the data completely unusable. Be sure this is what you want to do! Should you decide to erase a file, DBAS will guide you through the following procedure:

1. Specify whether you wish to erase an input file (data values only) or an output file (problem data plus results.)

2. Enter the name of the file to erase and press return.

2.2.6 CATALOG DATA DISK

CBS will provide a list of the files in "screen pages." You will have to press the enter key after viewing each screen page.

2.2.7 QUICK REVIEWS

Select Option #7 to view the QUICK REVIEW screens for each of the statistical analysis modules.

2.2.8 EXIT TO MAIN MENU

Select option #8 to return to the Main Program Menu.

2.2.9 EXIT TO DOS

Select option #9 to exit to DOS.

2.3 NON CBS DATA FILES

CBS 3.0 is now capable of inputting non-CBS ASCII based data files. The input procedure consists of a two step process. This procedure can be initiated after CBS indicates that the designated file is read using the standard input logic (i.e., number of groups, number of variables, number of data points per variable, data values and variable labels). If this step is unsuccessful, then the user is queried regarding the number of variables and the maximum number of data points per variable. An attempt is then made to read the actual data values from the designated file. If successful, the user can then use the data management module to "clean up" the data base.
input data file.

---

*A non-CBS data file must <u>not</u> contain any alpha numeric characters (e.g., A). Lotus based files must be saved using the text file option. (See Appendix G for details)

3.0 DESCRIPTIVE STATISTICS

3.1 PROGRAM DESCRIPTION:

CBS calculates a number of statistical measures for various data forms. The data may be in either raw or group form. A graphical display option is available for group data.

3.2 OVERVIEW

The use of data in business varies considerably from the strict measurements of financial performance to the more subjective assessment of customer preference. Typically, descriptive statistics are used to provide summary measures of collected data. In general, data is described using measures of central tendency and measures of variability. The standard measures of central tendency are the mean, median and mode. Specific measures of variability include the range, variance and standard deviation. Basically, data can be collected and analyzed in either raw or group form.

3.3 DATA INPUT

Problem data can be input from either terminal prompting or from a data file (see Chapter 2.0) The basic input includes:

◊ **Raw Data:**   The number of data points, the variable name and the data points (200 max).

◊ **Group Data:**   The number of groups (10 max). Each group requires a lower limit, upper limit and frequency count.

◊ **Data File Option:**
  • File name
  • Column name
  • Column number for variable of interest

3.4 MODEL OUTPUT

This program generates the following statistical measures for either raw or group data:

◊ **Mean:**   The sum of the data points divided by the number of data points.

◊ **Median:**   The point where 50 percent of the data values lie below and 50 percent lie above when the data is arrange in ascending order.

◊ **Mode:**   The most frequently occurring data value.

◊ **Modal Class:**   The class with the highest frequency count.

◊ **Range:**   The difference between the highest and lowest data values (Raw Data only).

◊ **Interval:**   The distance between each class (Group Data only).

◊ **Variance:**   A measure of variability around the mean.

◊ **Standard Deviation:**   The square root of the variance.

◊ **Coefficient of Skewness:**   The degree of the lack of symmetry of a data distribution.

◊ **Coefficient of Kurtosis:**   The degree of peakedness of a data distribution.

Note that the population variance/standard deviation and sample variance/standard deviation are slightly different. The denominator used in calculating the population variance is based on the on the total number of observations (n) whereas the denominator for calculating the sample variance is based on the total number of observations minus one (n-1).

3.5 DEMONSTRATION EXERCISES

EXERCISE #1: The general manager at Global Precious Metal Exchange is interested in analyzing changes in gold prices over the last year. The general manager has collected the following price data and wishes to determine the mean, median, mode, range, variance and standard deviation.

** PROMPTED INPUT **

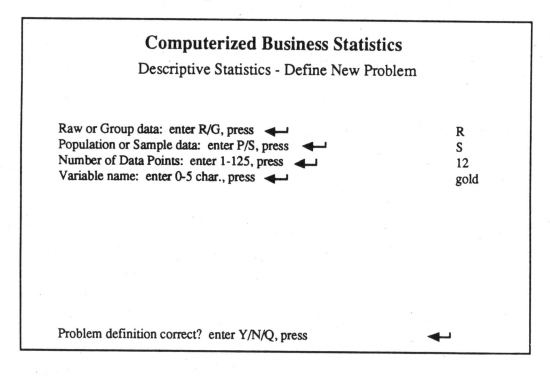

```
                 Computerized Business Statistics
                           MAIN MENU
                 1.      Exit to Operating System
                 2.      Data Base Management
                 3.      Descriptive Statistics
                 4.      Probability Theory
                 5.      Probability Distributions
                 6.      Survey Design
                 7.      Sampling and Estimation
                 8.      Hypothesis Testing
                 9.      Simple Correlation & Regression
                 10.     Multiple Regression Analysis
                 11.     Time Series and Forecasting
                 12.     Chi-Square Analysis
                 13.     Analysis of Variance
                 14.     NonParametric Methods
                 15.     Decision Analysis
                 16.     Statistical Quality Control

    Use arrow keys to move hi-lite bar to desired selection and press ◄─┘
```

Select: Enter Data from Keyboard to get to this next screen.

```
                 Computerized Business Statistics

            Descriptive Statistics - Define New Problem


    Raw or Group data: enter R/G, press ◄─┘            R
    Population or Sample data: enter P/S, press ◄─┘    S
    Number of Data Points: enter 1-125, press ◄─┘      12
    Variable name: enter 0-5 char., press ◄─┘          gold




    Problem definition correct? enter Y/N/Q, press      ◄─┘
```

19

Computerized Business Statistics

Table Commands: Enter Raw Data   Model:DSTA

Quick Mvmt			gold
F1	Row 1	1	371.30
F2	Row n	2	386.40
PgUp	Up 16	3	394.70
PgDn	Dn 16	4	382
L	Col 1	5	377.70
R	Col m	6	378.10
A	auto-adv	7	346.80
	(on)off	8	348.10
INS	add	9	341.30
	value	10	340.60
DEL	delete	11	341.50
	value	12	319.50
←→	Edit		
ESC	Restore		
	value		

	Mvmt	Press END	Enter Command OR Position Cursor & enter value for point
✛	↵	when Finished	Press ↵ to complete entry of value

To generate the results, press END to finish. At the Program Options Menu, select #7 Run Problem. The next prompt will be asking whether you want the data calculated as raw or group data. Raw data counts each value independently, while grouping the data allows you to separate your data into defined groups. For example, if you were using AGE as your variable, you may want to calculate statistics for age groupings such as ages 21-30, 31-40 and 41-50. This would be three groups at intervals of ten. To get the results below, respond to the 'convert raw to group' prompt with a N.

DESCRIPTIVE STATISTICS
** RESULTS **

CBS - Descriptive Statistics   I-GOLD   date/time

RESULTS

Mean:	360.6667
Median:	359.7000
Mode:	none
Range:	75.2000
Variance(s):	561.1553
Standard Deviations(s):	23.6887
Coefficient of Skewness:	-0.1203
Coefficient of Kurtosis:	1.4683

press   ↵

EXERCISE #2: The incoming freshman class (55 students) at Statistics University recently took a statistics proficiency examination. A brief inspection reveals that the scores range from 50 through 100 and are spread rather unevenly. The proctor decided to describe these results by grouping them into 5 categories as indicated in the following table. The proctor wishes to develop a set of descriptive statistics for these test scores.

SCORES	FREQUENCY
50 but *less* than 60	3
60 " " " 70	7
70 " " " 80	10
80 " " " 90	21
90 " " " 100	14

** DATA INPUT **

RAW OR GROUP DATA (R/G)? .... G

POPULATION OR SAMPLE (P/S)? .... S

NUMBER OF GROUPS (1 - 10)? 5

LOWER	UPPER	COUNT
50	60	3
60	70	7
70	80	10
80	90	21
90	100	14

** NOTE **

The range depicted in this data is FROM to the lower limit to *LESS THAN* the upper limit. This means that there were three scores in the 50 to 59 range, seven in the 60 to 69 range and so on.

DESCRIPTIVE STATISTICS
** RESULTS **

MEAN: ....81.5455   (Group average)

MEDIAN: ....83.3333   (Group midpoint)

MODAL CLASS: ....80 - 90   (Most frequently occurring group)

INTERVAL: 10   (Group width)

VARIANCE: ....134.1414   (Measure of variability around mean)

STANDARD DEV: ....11.5819   (Square root of variance)

COEFFICIENT OF SKEWNESS: ....-0.6514   (Lack of symetry of distribution)

COEFFICIENT OF KURTOSIS: ....2.5204   (Peakedness of distribution)

4.0 PROBABILITY THEORY

4.1 PROGRAM DESCRIPTION

This program contains the following three modules:

◊ **Counting Rules:**   Computes the number of permutations and combinations associated with a specified number of objects.

◊ **Probability Laws:**   Determines the probability of multiple events using the classical additive and multiplicative laws.

◊ **Bayesian Analysis:**   Computes posterior and marginal probabilities using prior probabilities and a conditional probability table.

4.2 OVERVIEW

The consequences of most managerial decisions are influenced by chance and uncertainty. The process of quantifying uncertainty is accomplished through the assignment of probability. Probability is a quantitative indicator of the chance that a certain event will occur and is measured on a scale from zero to one. A probability value of zero indicates that the event will not occur while a value of one indicates that the event will absolutely occur.

Counting rules provide one approach for developing probability values for well defined events. The basic idea is to count both the total number of different outcomes and the number of outcomes of interest for a given process. A probability value can then be determined by simply dividing the number of outcomes of interest by the total number of outcomes. Typically, permutations and combinations are used for counting processes involving a large number of outcomes. Permutations and combinations indicate the different ways objects can be classified. The basic difference between these two counting rules is that order is important in the case of permutations. For example, the sequence KKKAA is different than the sequence AAKKK in the case of a license plate (permutation) but the exactly the same in the case of the game of poker (combination).

Counting rules can be used for making probability assignments for single events. However, for multiple events several additional rules are required. The addition law is used to compute the probability for union of two or more events. The union of two or more events is the event that occurs if one or more of the events occur. The multiplication law is used to determine the probability for the intersection of two or more events. The intersection of two or more events is the event that occurs if all of the events occur. The relationship between events can be defined in terms of one of the following three conditions: independence, dependence or mutually exclusive. The nature of the relationship between events is required in order to apply either the additive or multiplicative law.

The process of revising probability estimates using additional information is known as Bayesian analysis and is used extensively in business decision analysis. Typically, management is interested in obtaining information on the future prior to making a decision. Quite often information regarding the future is obtained via sampling. In these cases, the sampling data is used to update the historical or prior probability estimates to provide a more accurate indicator of the future.

4.3 INPUT DATA

◊ Counting Rules

- Number of objects.
- Number of objects of interest.

◊ Probability Laws

- Number of events (2-3).
- Probability of each event.
- Nature of relationship between events:
  - Independent
  - Dependent (including the conditional probability value).
  - Mutually exclusive

◊ Bayesian Analysis

- Number of states (2-20).
- Number of indicators or predictors (2-20).
- Prior probabilities for each state.
- Conditional probability table (states and indicators).

4.4 MODEL OUTPUT

◊ Counting Rules

- Number of permutations of n objects.
- Number of permutations of n objects taken r at a time.
- Number of permutations of n objects with replacement.
- Number of combinations of n objects taken r at a time.
- Number of permutations of n objects with r distinct types of objects.

For numbers greater than 1.701E+38 the symbol >1.701E+38 will be reported. Additionally, output numbers greater than 1 million will be reported in scientific notation with six place accuracy, e.g., 1.00683 E+10. For the fifth model, the term "infeasible" will be reported in the event the sum of the individual r types does not equal the total number of n objects.

◊ Probability Laws

- The probability of the union of two or three events.
- The probability of the intersection of two or three events.

◊ Bayesian Analysis

- Indicator or marginal probabilities.
- Revised or posterior probabilities (matrix form).

EXERCISE #1: The director of the California Lottery wishes to determine the number of permutations and combinations associated with the game. The lottery process consists of drawing six balls from an urn containing 49 balls numbered 1 to 49. The following CBS screen illustrates the use of the counting rule model for determining the number of permutations and combinations for this problem.

Computerized Business Statistics

Probability Theory - Program Options Menu

> 0.   CBS Configuration
> **1.   Counting Rules**
> 2.   Probability Laws
> 3.   Bayesian Analysis
> 4.   Quick Reviews
> 5.   Exit to Main Menu
> 6.   Exit to Operating System

press ◄┘ to select option under hi-lite bar
press number or up/down arrow keys to move hi-lite bar

PROGRAM DEMONSTRATES THE USE OF COUNTING RULES,
PROBABILITY LAWS, AND BAYESIAN ANALYSIS

Computerized Business Statistics

Probability Theory - Counting Rules

			DATA INPUT PARAMETERS
1) $nPn = n!$	Number of permutations of n items.	$> 1.701E{+}38$	$n = ?49$
2) $nPn = n^r$	Number of permutations of n items with replacement.	$\approx 1.38412E{+}10$	$r = 6$
3) $nPr = \dfrac{n!}{(n\text{-}r)!}$	Number of permutations of n items taken r items at a time	$\approx 1.00683E{+}10$	$x1 = 0$ $x2 = 0$
4) $nCr = \dfrac{n!}{r!(n\text{-}r)!}$	Number of combinations of n items taken r items at a time.	$\approx 1.39838E{+}07$	$x3 = 0$ $x4 = 0$
5) $nPx1...xr = \dfrac{n!}{x1!..xr!}$	Number of permutations of n items, x1 of type 1, x2 of type 2, etc. for r different types.	$\Sigma x = 0$ infeasible	$x5 = 0$ $x6 = 0$

Enter value for applicable parameters and press C to calculate, END to finish,
or P to print. The up and down arrows move the cursor between parameters.

These results show that there is a little over 10 billion different possible permutations and almost 14 million combinations in the California Lottery. Clearly, the chances of winning the lottery based on permutations is too small for the target California adult population of 15 million. This is why the lottery is based on combinations.

EXERCISE #2: The director of the California "Big Spin" is interested in determining the probability that one of two contestants or both will win $1 million. The chances of winning $1 million on a single spin of the wheel is 0.08. The following CBS screen illustrates the use of the probability laws model in determining the probability that one or both of the contestants will win $1 million. This problem can be solved by selecting option #2 (Probability Laws) from the Program Options Menu.

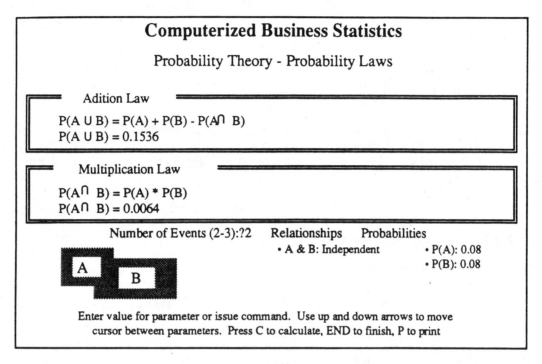

Computerized Business Statistics

Probability Theory - Probability Laws

Adition Law

$P(A \cup B) = P(A) + P(B) - P(A \cap B)$
$P(A \cup B) = 0.1536$

Multiplication Law

$P(A \cap B) = P(A) * P(B)$
$P(A \cap B) = 0.0064$

Number of Events (2-3):?2   Relationships   Probabilities
• A & B: Independent   • P(A): 0.08
                            • P(B): 0.08

A
B

Enter value for parameter or issue command. Use up and down arrows to move cursor between parameters. Press C to calculate, END to finish, P to print

The above analysis is based on the assumption that each spin of the wheel is independent of any other spin. In this case, the appropriate relationship is to select independent. These results show that there is an approximate 15% chance (additive law) that one of the two contestants will win $1 million and only a 0.0064 chance (multiplication law) that both contestants will win $1 million on a single spin.

EXERCISE #3: The U.S. Weather Service has recently placed in orbit a satellite designed to improve weather prediction throughout the continental United States. Initially, the satellite will be limited to predicting the occurrence of rainfall in a given area. The recorded accuracy of the satellite is reported in the following conditional table. For example, the satellite successfully predicted rain 90% of the time when it actually rained.

** SATELLITE INDICATOR **

		Rain	No Rain
	RAIN (S1)	0.9	0.1
STATE	OVERCAST (S2)	0.5	0.5
	CLEAR (S3)	0.2	0.8

The manager of the local weather service would like to know the chances of various weather patterns occurring given a specific prediction from the satellite. The historical data for this area reveals, that for this time of the year, it rains 30% of the time, is cloudy 50% of the time and is clear 20% of the time.

** PROMPTED INPUT **

NUMBER OF STATES (Rows: 1 TO 20) ? 3

NUMBER OF INDICATORS (Columns: 1 TO 20) ?.......................2

CONDITIONAL PROBABILITY TABLE

	I1	I2
S1?	0.9	0.1
S2?	0.5	0.5
S3?	0.2	0.8

PRIOR PROBABILITIES

S1 (0 TO 1) ? 3
S2 (0 TO 1) ? 5
S3 (0 TO 1) ? 2

BAYESIAN ANALYSIS
** RESULTS **

PREDICTION   MARGINAL PROBABILITIES

        1   0.5600
        2   0.4300

REVISED PROBABILITIES

PREDICTOR   1   2   3

        1   0.4821   0.4464   0.0714
        2   0.0682   0.5682   0.3636

An analysis of these results shows that there is a 0.5682 chance that the satellite will indicate rain. Furthermore, there is a 0.3636 chance that the weather will be clear, given a forecast of no rain from the satellite.

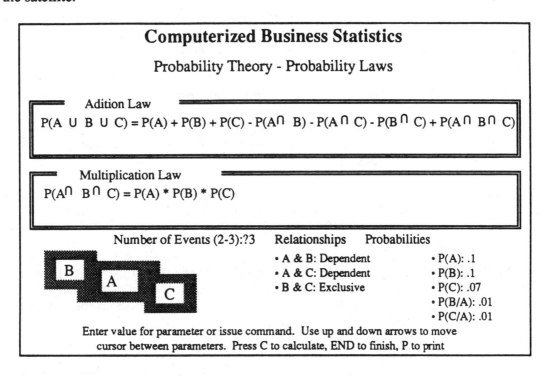

Computerized Business Statistics

Probability Theory - Probability Laws

Adition Law

$P(A \cup B \cup C) = P(A) + P(B) + P(C) - P(A \cap B) - P(A \cap C) - P(B \cap C) + P(A \cap B \cap C)$

Multiplication Law

$P(A \cap B \cap C) = P(A) * P(B) * P(C)$

Number of Events (2-3):?3   Relationships   Probabilities

• A & B: Dependent   • P(A): .1
• A & C: Dependent   • P(B): .1
• B & C: Exclusive   • P(C): .07
                          • P(B/A): .01
                          • P(C/A): .01

Enter value for parameter or issue command. Use up and down arrows to move cursor between parameters. Press C to calculate, END to finish, P to print

5.0 PROBABILITY FUNCTIONS

5.1 PROGRAM DESCRIPTION

This program determines probability values for seven of the most frequently used probability functions: Binomial, Poisson, Hypergeometric, Normal, t, F and chi-square. Both point and range probability estimates are provided by the program. Each of the distributions is supported by a graphics package.

5.2 OVERVIEW

Probability considerations are central to the managerial decision making process. Probability analysis would not be needed if the results of alternative decisions were known with certainty. However, there is no such thing as certainty in business. Probability is the chance something will happen. A zero (0) probability indicates that the event will never happen; a one (1) indicates that the event it will always happen. Thus, probability expressions will vary between 0 and 1 and are usually expressed as a fraction or a percentage.

Classical probability is defined as the number of times an event will occur divided by the total number of possible events. The more useful definition is one which rests on relative frequency. Thus, probability is defined as the proportion of the time that an event will occur over a large number of attempts.

This program contains the following seven probability distributions:

1. Binomial: A discrete distribution based on a specific number of trials involving two possible outcomes where the probability of an individual outcome is constant.

2. Poisson: A discrete distribution where the probability of occurrence is the same for any two intervals and the events are independent. The Poisson distribution is described by a single parameter often known as the arrival rate

3. Hypergeometric: A discrete distribution based on a specific number of trials involving two possible outcomes where the probability of an event changes from trial to trial. This distribution is used to describe processes that involve sampling without replacement.

4. Normal: A distribution of continuous values with a single peak and tails extending indefinitely in both directions from the center line and described by the mean and standard deviation. The standard normal distribution is a special form of the normal curve with a mean of zero and a standard deviation of one.

5. t: A family of continuous distributions with a single centerline peak with tails extending indefinitely in both directions from the center line and described by a mean of zero and a standard deviation based on the sample size. The t distribution approaches the normal curve as the sample size becomes large (30 or larger).

6. F:	A family of continuous distributions described by two parameters: degrees of freedom of the numerator and degrees of freedom of the denominator. Generally speaking, the F distribution is used in testing hypothesis regarding variances. The F distribution approaches the normal curve as the degrees of freedom for both parameters becomes large.
7. Chi -square:	A family of continuous distribution described by the degrees of freedom. This distribution is used primarily to test hypothesis regarding goodness of fit and variable independence. The chi-square distribution is a special case of the F distribution.

5.3 DATA INPUT

◊ Binomial distribution:	Number of trials and probability of occurrence of a single event.
◊ Poisson distribution:	Average occurrence rate.
◊ Hypergeometric distribution:	Population size, number of events of interest in the population, and sample size.
◊ Normal distribution:	Mean and standard deviation.
◊ t distribution:	Mean, standard deviation and degrees of freedom.
◊ F distribution:	Degrees of freedom for the numerator and degrees of freedom for the denominator.
◊ Chi-square distribution:	Degrees of freedom.

5.4 MODEL OUTPUT

The model output provides both point and range probability estimates for the problem of interest. Each of the probability distributions contained in this program are highlighted in the next section.

5.5 DEMONSTRATION EXERCISES

EXERCISE #1: An outside auditor hired by the Johnson Pharmaceutical Company has randomly selected five accounts receivable. If three percent of all accounts contain an error, what is the probability that the auditor finds one or more accounts in error?

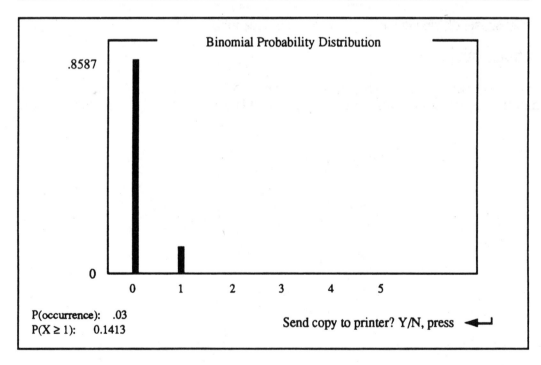

Computerized Business Statistics

Probability Distributions - Program Options Menu

OPTIONS	------- FUNCTIONS -------		
1) BINOMIAL	$P(x \geq a)$	$P(x = a)$	$P(a \leq x \leq b)$
2) POISSON	$P(x \geq a)$	$P(x = a)$	$P(a \leq x \leq b)$
3) HYPERGEOMETRIC	$P(x \geq a)$	$P(x = a)$	$P(a \leq x \leq b)$
4) NORMAL	$P(x \geq a)$	$P(mean \leq x \leq a)$	$P(a \leq x \leq b)$
5) t	$P(x \geq a)$	$P(mean \leq x \leq a)$	$P(a \leq x \leq b)$
6) F	$P(x \geq a)$		
7) CHI-SQUARE	$P(x \geq a)$		
8) QUICK REVIEWS			
9) EXIT TO MAIN MENU			
10) EXIT TO OPERATING SYSTEM			

-- Input Data --

Enter number of trials (2-30000) and press ⏎   5
Enter probability of an ocurance (0-1) and press ⏎   .03
Enter number of occurances (0-5) and press ⏎   1

Binomial Probability Distribution

.8587

0

      0   1   2   3   4   5

P(occurrence):   .03
$P(X \geq 1)$:   0.1413

Send copy to printer? Y/N, press ⏎

30

EXERCISE #2: The general manager of the Western Telephone Exchange is concerned about the rate of line failures on the company's new fiber optics network. The network is experiencing a line failure rate of three per 100 miles of network per month. The general manager would like to know the probability that two or more line failures per 100 miles will occur this month.

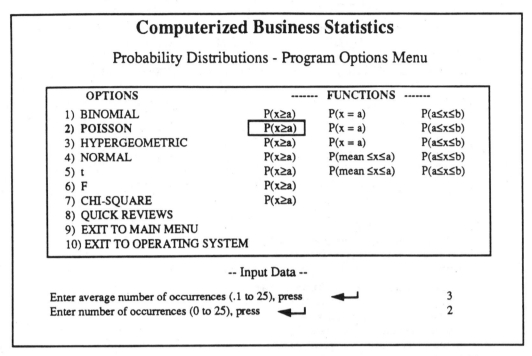

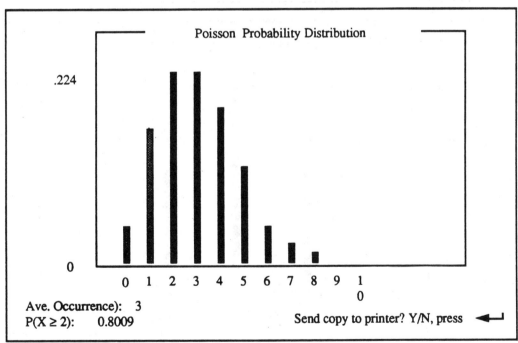

EXERCISE #3: The district attorney for Los Angeles County would like to for a grand jury of four members from a pool of 20 pre-screened voting age adults, 10 from the minority community. The district attorney would like to know the probability that the panel will be composed of at least two minority citizens (assume that 50% of the population is minority). This problem can be solved using the hypergeometric distribution (option #3).

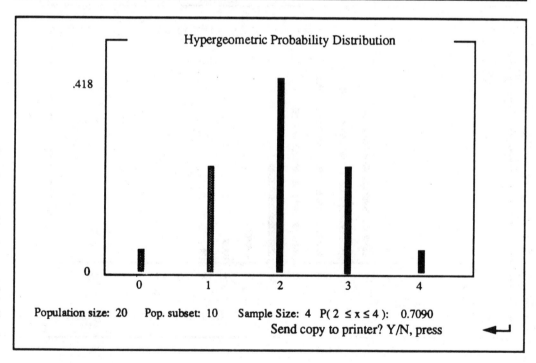

Computerized Business Statistics

Probability Distributions - Program Options Menu

OPTIONS	------- FUNCTIONS -------		
1) BINOMIAL	$P(x \geq a)$	$P(x = a)$	$P(a \leq x \leq b)$
2) POISSON	$P(x \geq a)$	$P(x = a)$	$P(a \leq x \leq b)$
3) HYPERGEOMETRIC	$P(x \geq a)$	$P(x = a)$	$\boxed{P(a \leq x \leq b)}$
4) NORMAL	$P(x \geq a)$	$P(\text{mean} \leq x \leq a)$	$P(a \leq x \leq b)$
5) t	$P(x \geq a)$	$P(\text{mean} \leq x \leq a)$	$P(a \leq x \leq b)$
6) F	$P(x \geq a)$		
7) CHI-SQUARE	$P(x \geq a)$		
8) QUICK REVIEWS			
9) EXIT TO MAIN MENU			
10) EXIT TO OPERATING SYSTEM			

-- Input Data --

Enter population size (1 to 33), press ⏎	20
Enter size of population subset (1 to 20), press ⏎	10
Enter sample size (1 to 20), press ⏎	4
Enter lower limit (0 to 4), press ⏎	2
Enter upper limit (2 to 4), press ⏎	4

Hypergeometric Probability Distribution

.418

0

0   1   2   3   4

Population size: 20   Pop. subset: 10   Sample Size: 4   P(2 ≤ x ≤ 4):   0.7090

Send copy to printer? Y/N, press ⏎

32

EXERCISE #4: The manager at Seven-Day Tire Company recently reviewed the mileage results from last year's sales. The average mileage before replacement was 30,000 miles with a standard deviation of 5,000 miles. The manager would like to know the probability that a tire will achieve at least 25,000 miles before replacement. This problem can be solved using the normal distribution (option #4).

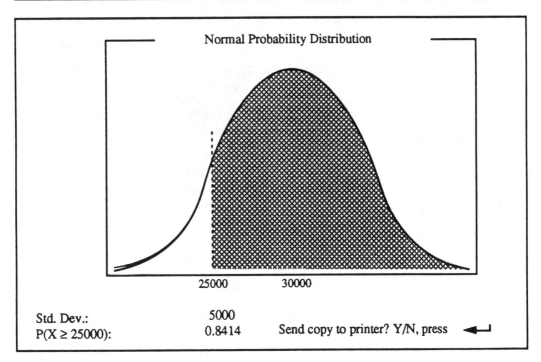

Computerized Business Statistics

Probability Distributions - Program Options Menu

OPTIONS		------ FUNCTIONS ------	
1) BINOMIAL	$P(x \geq a)$	$P(x = a)$	$P(a \leq x \leq b)$
2) POISSON	$P(x \geq a)$	$P(x = a)$	$P(a \leq x \leq b)$
3) HYPERGEOMETRIC	$P(x \geq a)$	$P(x = a)$	$P(a \leq x \leq b)$
4) NORMAL	$P(x \geq a)$	$P(\text{mean} \leq x \leq a)$	$P(a \leq x \leq b)$
5) t	$P(x \geq a)$	$P(\text{mean} \leq x \leq a)$	$P(a \leq x \leq b)$
6) F	$P(x \geq a)$		
7) CHI-SQUARE	$P(x \geq a)$		
8) QUICK REVIEWS			
9) EXIT TO MAIN MENU			
10) EXIT TO OPERATING SYSTEM			

-- Input Data --

Enter mean, press ◄┘	30000
Enter standard deviation ($\geq$0), press ◄┘	5000
Enter A, press ◄┘	25000

Normal Probability Distribution

25000   30000

Std. Dev.:	5000	
$P(X \geq 25000)$:	0.8414	Send copy to printer? Y/N, press ◄┘

33

EXERCISE #5: The production manager at Ampex Manufacturing has recent collected data on machinery downtime. The manager found in a sample of 10 machines an average downtime of 32 hours per quarter with a standard deviation of 12 hours per quarter. The manager would like to know the chances that the downtime for a machine will range between 30 to 40 hours. This problem can be solved using the t distribution (option #5).

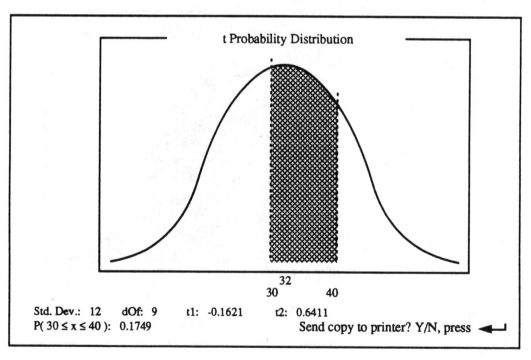

Computerized Business Statistics

Probability Distributions - Program Options Menu

OPTIONS	------- FUNCTIONS -------		
1) BINOMIAL	$P(x \geq a)$	$P(x = a)$	$P(a \leq x \leq b)$
2) POISSON	$P(x \geq a)$	$P(x = a)$	$P(a \leq x \leq b)$
3) HYPERGEOMETRIC	$P(x \geq a)$	$P(x = a)$	$P(a \leq x \leq b)$
4) NORMAL	$P(x \geq a)$	$P(mean \leq x \leq a)$	$P(a \leq x \leq b)$
5) t	$P(x \geq a)$	$P(mean \leq x \leq a)$	$\boxed{P(a \leq x \leq b)}$
6) F	$P(x \geq a)$		
7) CHI-SQUARE	$P(x \geq a)$		
8) QUICK REVIEWS			
9) EXIT TO MAIN MENU			
10) EXIT TO OPERATING SYSTEM			

-- Input Data --

Enter mean, press ◄──┘	32
Enter standard deviation (≥ 0), press ◄──┘	12
Enter lower limit (A), press ◄──┘	30
Enter upper limit (B >= 30), press ◄──┘	40
Enter degrees of freedom (1 to 300), press ◄──┘	9

t Probability Distribution

32
30   40

Std. Dev.: 12   dOf: 9   t1: -0.1621   t2: 0.6411
P(30 ≤ x ≤ 40): 0.1749   Send copy to printer? Y/N, press ◄──┘

EXERCISE #6: Use the F distribution to determine the probability of a random variable is greater-than-or-equal-to four given twenty degrees of freedom for the numerator and eight degrees of freedom for the denominator (option #6).

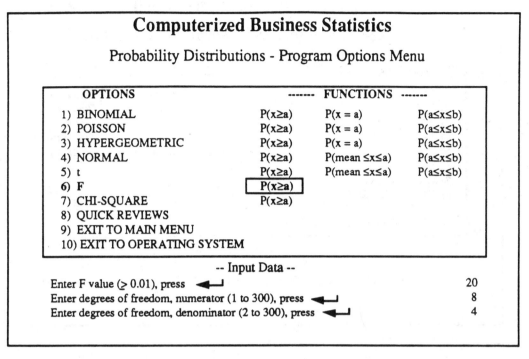

Computerized Business Statistics

Probability Distributions - Program Options Menu

OPTIONS	------ FUNCTIONS ------		
1) BINOMIAL	$P(x \geq a)$	$P(x = a)$	$P(a \leq x \leq b)$
2) POISSON	$P(x \geq a)$	$P(x = a)$	$P(a \leq x \leq b)$
3) HYPERGEOMETRIC	$P(x \geq a)$	$P(x = a)$	$P(a \leq x \leq b)$
4) NORMAL	$P(x \geq a)$	$P(mean \leq x \leq a)$	$P(a \leq x \leq b)$
5) t	$P(x \geq a)$	$P(mean \leq x \leq a)$	$P(a \leq x \leq b)$
6) F	$\boxed{P(x \geq a)}$		
7) CHI-SQUARE	$P(x \geq a)$		
8) QUICK REVIEWS			
9) EXIT TO MAIN MENU			
10) EXIT TO OPERATING SYSTEM			

-- Input Data --

Enter F value (≥ 0.01), press ⏎   20
Enter degrees of freedom, numerator (1 to 300), press ⏎   8
Enter degrees of freedom, denominator (2 to 300), press ⏎   4

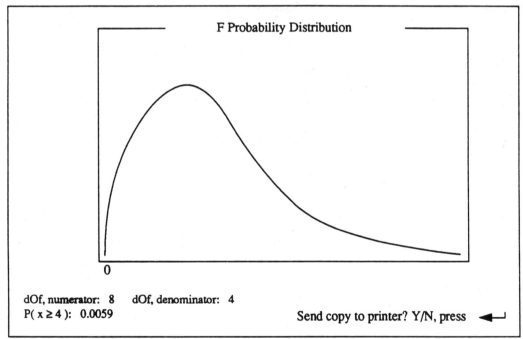

F Probability Distribution

0

dOf, numerator: 8   dOf, denominator: 4
$P(x \geq 4)$: 0.0059   Send copy to printer? Y/N, press ⏎

EXERCISE #7: Use the chi-square distribution to determine the probability that the value of a random variable is greater-than-or-equal-to 21 given 12 degrees of freedom (option #7).

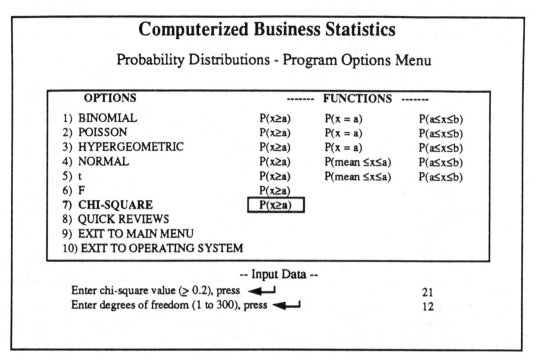

Computerized Business Statistics

Probability Distributions - Program Options Menu

OPTIONS	------- FUNCTIONS -------		
1) BINOMIAL	$P(x \geq a)$	$P(x = a)$	$P(a \leq x \leq b)$
2) POISSON	$P(x \geq a)$	$P(x = a)$	$P(a \leq x \leq b)$
3) HYPERGEOMETRIC	$P(x \geq a)$	$P(x = a)$	$P(a \leq x \leq b)$
4) NORMAL	$P(x \geq a)$	$P(mean \leq x \leq a)$	$P(a \leq x \leq b)$
5) t	$P(x \geq a)$	$P(mean \leq x \leq a)$	$P(a \leq x \leq b)$
6) F	$P(x \geq a)$		
7) CHI-SQUARE	$P(x \geq a)$		
8) QUICK REVIEWS			
9) EXIT TO MAIN MENU			
10) EXIT TO OPERATING SYSTEM			

-- Input Data --

Enter chi-square value ($\geq$ 0.2), press ◄┘   21
Enter degrees of freedom (1 to 300), press ◄┘   12

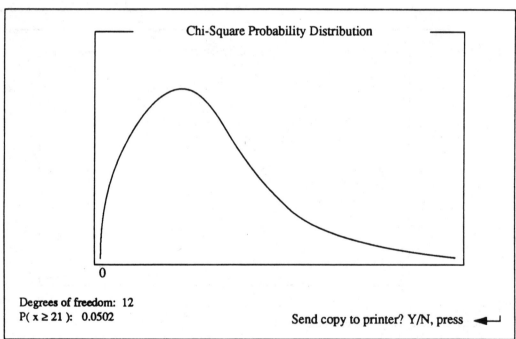

Chi-Square Probability Distribution

0

Degrees of freedom: 12
$P(x \geq 21)$: 0.0502

Send copy to printer? Y/N, press ◄┘

6.0 SURVEY DESIGN

6.1 PROGRAM DESCRIPTION

This program is designed to assist the user in preparing a survey of up to 20 questions. Each question is treated as an item with specific attributes, e.g., type of response, number of categories, left margin. A number of standard question are available which can be integrated with questions developed by the user. Formulated questions can be modified during the developmental process. The developed questionnaire can be printed out or stored on a data disk for subsequent use or modification.

6.2 OVERVIEW

Survey questionnaires are playing an ever increasing role in the formulation of both public and private sector policies. Typically, the design of a questionnaire consists of following six basic steps:

1. Specifying the primary purpose
2. Setting specific objectives
3. Formulating a sample plan
4. Formulating the questions, i.e., item construction
5. Selecting the measurement scales
6. Carrying out a pre-test of the developed survey instrument

Two of the most time consuming and difficult tasks are item construction and selecting the most appropriate response scale. This program is designed to support both of these tasks.

6.3 DATA INPUT

The input/editing level screens are designed to display prior responses.
There can be up to three layers of activity visible at one time. The limit case would be the display of question(s) starting at the top of the screen, partially covered by input/edit of an individual question starting in the middle of the screen, partially covered by the input options menu on the bottom of the screen. Menus, prompts and input instructions always appear at the bottom of the screen.

The input options menu contains the following options:

N=New	C=Copy	E=Edit	T=Title	F=Finish
S=Standard	D=Delete	R=Reorder	V=View	Q=Quit

N=New This option permits formulating a new question. A new question is automatically placed at the end of the questionnaire.

S=Standard This option permits selecting one of the standard questions or responses stored in the program. This option can not be executed if questionnaire already has 20 questions. The selected question is automatically placed at the end of the questionnaire.

C=Copy   This option produces a copy of an item already in the questionnaire. The procedure can be terminated at either step by inputting 0. The copy command can not be executed if the survey already has 20 questions. Additionally, the copy command can not be used when all of the user-definable text question storage space is already used.

D=Delete This option removes a specific question from the survey. Procedure has two steps: 1) select question to delete, 2) confirm. The procedure can be terminated at either step by inputting a 0. The program automatically reorders the remaining questions.

E=Edit   This option allows for the editing of select question.

R=Reorder This option allows for reordering the survey. There are two steps: 1) select question to move, 2) select new position. The procedure can be terminated at either step by inputting a 0.

T=Title   This option permits creating or editing a title (up to 70 characters) and the number of lines between each question. Press the up and down arrows to switch fields. Press END to return to the input options menu.

V=View   This option Displays as many questions as will fit on screen starting with a given question.

F=Finish This option permits saving questionnaire on a separate data diskette. A saved questionnaire can be recalled for subsequent modification.

Q=Quit   This option returns to the main program menu without saving current survey.

Each item contain three basic elements: A question, a response type, and a left margin for displaying the response portion of the item. A question may be between 0 and 255 characters.

There are five response types:

    0 = none (response is assumed to be imbedded in the question)

    1 = numeric scale

    2 = numeric categories

    3 = text categories

    4 = open ended

Selection of the desired response is made by using the left and right arrow keys. Response types 1 through 3 have additional attributes: number of categories (1-10), blank size for response(5-25), label size for category description (5-25), and display style for categories (across or down). The left margin may be between 1 and 20 spaces.

6.4 OUTPUT

The survey design module features three output options: screen, printer and disk. Screen output is like the view mode but does not permit deviation from straight sequential listing of the questions. A printer option is available for producing a hardcopy. Disk file is primarily designed for exporting the developed questionnaire to a word processor, or storing for later printing. An output disk file questionnaire can not be loaded for editing.

6.5 DEMONSTRATION EXERCISES

6.5.1 Standard Survey

The following example survey (selection 3 on main menu) presents each of the standard questions stored within the program:

1. Your age:
   - _____ 20 <
   - _____ 20 to 39
   - _____ 60 to 79
   - _____ 80 to 99
   - _____ 100 +

2. Your sex:

       Male   Female

   | _____ | | _____ |

3. Your Income:
   - _____ 15000 <
   - _____ 15000 to 29999
   - _____ 30000 to 44999
   - _____ 45000 to 59999
   - _____ 60000 +

4. Number of years at your present address:
   - _____ 1 <
   - _____ 1 to 3
   - _____ 4 to 6
   - _____ 7 to 9
   - _____ 10 +

5. Highest Level of Education:
   - _____ Grade School
   - _____ High School
   - _____ Undergraduate Degree
   - _____ Masters Degree
   - _____ Doctoral Degree

6. Race:

_____	Caucasian
_____	Hispanic
_____	Black
_____	Oriental
_____	American Indian
_____	Other

7.

Strongly Agree	Agree	Undecided	Disagree	Strongly Disagree
|_____|	|_____|	|_____|	|_____|	|_____|

8.

Better	Same	Worse
|_____|	|_____|	|_____|

9.

_____	Agree
_____	Disagree

10.

_____

_____

_____

6.5.2 California Health Spa

The following exercise, involving a survey of current members of the California Health Spa, is presented to illustrate the use of this program.

Press 1 for new survey at program options menu.

Fill in the following values:

Title: MEMBERSHIP SURVEY
Lines between questions: 1
Press F

Press S to add standard question
Standard Question number: 1

Press S to add standard question
Standard Question number: 2

Press S to add standard question
Standard Question number: 3

Press N to add new question
Fill in values
Question: Number of years you have attended the spa? _____
Response type: none
Press S to store question
press F

Press S to add standard question
Standard Question number: 7
Press S to add standard question
Standard Question number: 7

Press E to edit
Question number: 5
add to Question text: I believe that the spa's facilities are adequate.
press S to store question
press N for next question

add to Question text: I believe that the spa's training programs are adequate.
press S to store question
press F

Press A to add question
fill in values
Question: Please rank the following spa's services in terms of your interest:
Response Type: text categories
Left Indent: 1. Increase operating hours.
Number of Categories: 4   2. Increase Locker room area.
Blank size   3. Expand Running Track.
label size   4. Add Weight Training Class.
Press S to store question
press F

Press A to add question
Question: Please provide any additional comments regarding your experience at the spa.
Response Type: open-ended
Number of lines: 3
Left indent:
Press S to store question
Press F

press F to return to Survey Program Options Menu
Press 7 to generate survey
Press S to view on screen

7.0 SAMPLING AND ESTIMATION

7.1 PROGRAM DESCRIPTION

This program contains the following four options:

1. Generates random numbers.
2. Demonstrates the central limit theorem.
3. Determines sample size based on an acceptable level of error.
4. Computes confidence intervals for either raw or summary data.

A graphics package is available for illustrating the central limit theorem.

7.2 OVERVIEW

The concept of randomness is basic to modern statistical analysis. Simply stated, the notion of randomness indicates that every event or sample has an equal opportunity of occurring. Thus, the most effective means for obtaining a representative sample(s) from a population is to sample randomly.

The central limit theorem is the most important theoretical concept in modern statistical inference. The central limit theorem can be stated as follows:

The sampling distribution of the mean of a random variable drawn from a population approaches a normal distribution as the sample size increases regardless of the shape of the population distribution.

The basic significance of the central limit theorem is that inferences about population parameters can be made without knowing the shape or characteristics of the population.

A key aspect in the data collection process is in determining the optimal sample size. The basic tradeoff in selecting the appropriate sample size involves costs versus accuracy. On the one hand, a survey based on a very small sample can yield misleading or incorrect results. On the other hand, a survey which uses a very large a sample can be expensive and still may not yield more meaningful results than one using a more moderately sized sample. Typically ,two methods are available for determining sample size based on the desired level of accuracy. One approach uses a combination of alpha and sampling errors while the other uses a combination of alpha and beta errors.

Confidence intervals are important in the sampling process because they provide additional insight into the precision of the developed estimates. Typically, a point estimate (e.g., mean) does not provide information regarding accuracy of the estimate. Furthermore, a point estimate does not provide an exact value of the population parameter. An interval estimate, on the other hand, provides a range of values wherein the population parameter most likely lies. A confidence interval for means is a function of the sample mean, the sample standard deviation, the sample size and the desired level of confidence. Confidence intervals for proportions are developed in a similar manner. Usually, confidence intervals are reported in in terms of a statistical statement. For example, the R&D manager is 95% confident that the actual operating life of the new product falls between 34 and 48 months. This model can develop confidence intervals for simple, cluster or stratified samples. A maximum of five cluster or stratified categories are permitted

7.3 DATA INPUT

OPTION	REQUIREMENT
1. Random Numbers:	The number of random numbers required.
2. Central Limit :	The size of the sample.
3. Sample Size;	The standard deviation, the level of significance (i.e., alpha), and either the sampling error or the beta error and alternative hypothesis.
4. Confidence Interval:	Raw data or summary statistics (mean and standard deviation), sample size, and level of significance.

7.4 MODEL OUTPUT

This program generates the following output depending on the option selected:

◊ Random Numbers (1 to 100 five digit numbers).

◊ Normal Distribution (histogram and frequency table).

◊ Sample Size.

◊ Confidence Intervals:

- Simple
- Cluster
- Stratified

43

7.5 DEMONSTRATION EXERCISES

EXERCISE #1: Generate 40 random numbers.

```
┌─────────────────────────────────────────────────────────────┐
│              Computerized Business Statistics                 │
│                                                               │
│         Sampling and Estimation - Program Options Menu        │
│                                                               │
│   ┌───────────────────────────────────────────────────────┐ │
│   │    0.   CBS Configuration                               │ │
│   │   ┌──────────────────────────────────────────────────┐ │ │
│   │   │ 1.   Generate Random Numbers                      │ │ │
│   │   └──────────────────────────────────────────────────┘ │ │
│   │    2.   Central Limit Theorem Demonstration             │ │
│   │    3.   Compute Sample Size                             │ │
│   │    4.   Interval Estimation                            │ │
│   │    5.   Quick Reviews                                  │ │
│   │    6.   Exit to Main Menu                              │ │
│   │    7.   Exit to Operating System                       │ │
│   │                                                        │ │
│   └───────────────────────────────────────────────────────┘ │
│                                                               │
│          press  ◄─┘  to select option under hi-lite bar      │
│       press number or up/down arrow keys to move hi-lite bar  │
│                                                               │
│   PROGRAM GENERATES RANDOM NUMBERS, DEMONSTRATES THE CENTRAL LIMIT │
│   THEOREM, DETERMINES SAMPLE SIZES, AND COMPUTES INTERVAL ESTIMATES │
└─────────────────────────────────────────────────────────────┘
```

SELECT OPTION (1 - 7):...1

NUMBER OF RANDOM DIGITS (1 - 100):...............................40

** RANDOM NUMBERS **

	1	2	3	4
1.	77793	55183	51738	19782
2.	96846	81410	69992	02705
3.	80878	12323	48529	91429
4.	53683	57325	12321	60394
5.	28322	98134	58149	27330
6.	27061	79497	33222	35240
7.	78947	84511	72194	62871
8.	71248	69848	49830	55874
9.	15048	16903	18567	49804
10.	25774	37729	41756	81251

EXERCISE #2: Develop a sampling distribution for a sample size of 15.

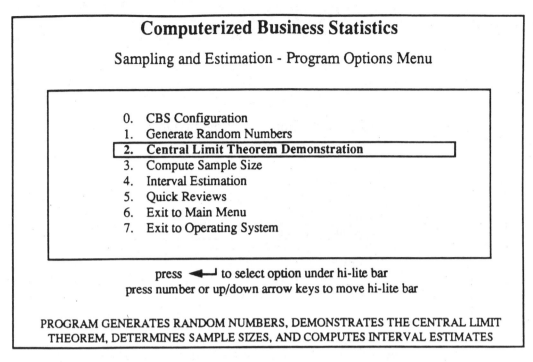

Computerized Business Statistics

Sampling and Estimation - Program Options Menu

0. CBS Configuration
1. Generate Random Numbers
2. **Central Limit Theorem Demonstration**
3. Compute Sample Size
4. Interval Estimation
5. Quick Reviews
6. Exit to Main Menu
7. Exit to Operating System

press ◄─┘ to select option under hi-lite bar
press number or up/down arrow keys to move hi-lite bar

PROGRAM GENERATES RANDOM NUMBERS, DEMONSTRATES THE CENTRAL LIMIT
THEOREM, DETERMINES SAMPLE SIZES, AND COMPUTES INTERVAL ESTIMATES

SELECT OPTION (1-7): 2

SAMPLE SIZE (1 - 99): 15

The following presents a CBS generated frequency distribution based on randomly selecting a
sample of size 15 from a uniform distribution. Generally speaking, the frequency distribution will
take on the shape of a normal curve as the sample size increases.

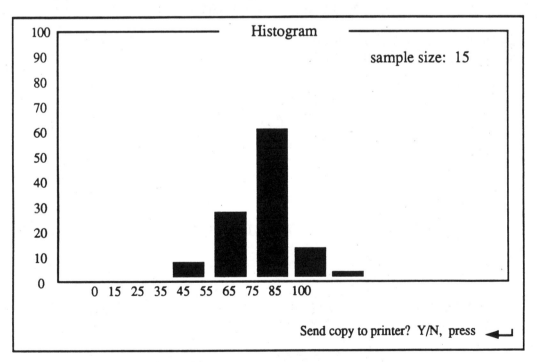

Histogram

sample size: 15

Send copy to printer? Y/N, press ◄─┘

45

EXERCISE #3: The estimated average use life for Hilight Corporation's standard spark plug is 500 hours. The estimated population standard deviation is 50 hours. The projected actual mean use life for the last production batch is 475 hours. The management wishes to select a random sample from the last batch, based on an alpha error of 5% and a beta error of 10%. What is the appropriate sample size?

```
╔══════════════════════════════════════════════════════════════╗
║              Computerized Business Statistics                  ║
║                                                                ║
║          Sampling and Estimation - Program Options Menu        ║
║                                                                ║
║    ┌────────────────────────────────────────────────────┐     ║
║    │                                                      │     ║
║    │      0.  CBS Configuration                           │     ║
║    │      1.  Generate Random Numbers                     │     ║
║    │      2.  Central Limit Theorem Demonstration         │     ║
║    │     ┌────────────────────────────────────────────┐   │    ║
║    │     │ 3.  Compute Sample Size                     │   │    ║
║    │     └────────────────────────────────────────────┘   │    ║
║    │      4.  Interval Estimation                         │     ║
║    │      5.  Quick Reviews                               │     ║
║    │      6.  Exit to Main Menu                           │     ║
║    │      7.  Exit to Operating System                    │     ║
║    │                                                      │     ║
║    └────────────────────────────────────────────────────┘     ║
║                                                                ║
║         press ◄──┘ to select option under hi-lite bar          ║
║       press number or up/down arrow keys to move hi-lite bar   ║
║                                                                ║
║   PROGRAM GENERATES RANDOM NUMBERS, DEMONSTRATES THE CENTRAL    ║
║   LIMIT THEOREM, DETERMINES SAMPLE SIZES, AND COMPUTES          ║
║   INTERVAL ESTIMATES                                           ║
╚══════════════════════════════════════════════════════════════╝
```

SELECT OPTION (1-7): 3

** SAMPLE SIZE ANALYSIS **

1. Sample size from Alpha/Beta Error
2. Sample size from Sampling Error

   Enter Option (1-2) 1

** DATA TYPE **

1. Means
2. Proportions

   Enter Option (1-2) 1

** DATA INPUT **

STANDARD DEVIATION: ....50 hours
ALPHA ERROR (TYPE I): 0.05
BETA ERROR (TYPE II): 0.10
POPULATION HYPOTHESIS VALUE: 500
ALTERNATIVE HYPOTHESIS VALUE: 475

** SAMPLE SIZE = 52 **

EXERCISE #4: Wilcox Corporation provides temporary accounting professionals for small to medium businesses operating throughout California. The job scheduling manager has received a number of complaints from several of the company's best customers regarding the seemingly high rate of absenteeism among Wilcox employees. A sample of 30 employee records taken at random revealed an absent rate of 44.20 hours with a standard deviation of 21.08 hours over the last year.

Computerized Business Statistics

Sampling and Estimation - Program Options Menu

0. CBS Configuration
1. Generate Random Numbers
2. Central Limit Theorem Demonstration
3. Compute Sample Size
4. **Interval Estimation**
5. Quick Reviews
6. Exit to Main Menu
7. Exit to Operating System

press ◄─┘ to select option under hi-lite bar
press number or up/down arrow keys to move hi-lite bar

PROGRAM GENERATES RANDOM NUMBERS, DEMONSTRATES THE CENTRAL LIMIT
THEOREM, DETERMINES SAMPLE SIZES, AND COMPUTES INTERVAL ESTIMATES

SELECT OPTION (1 - 7): ....4......

At the Interval Estimation program options menu, select option #1, "Enter Data from Keyboard" to proceed with this exercise.

Computerized Business Statistics

Interval Estimation - Set Up New Problem

Data Type:	[R]Raw	[S]Summary	S
Data Form:	[M]Means	[P]Proportions	M
Proportion data consists of values from 0 to 1.			
Population:	[1]One Population	[2]Two Populations	1
	[U]Unmatched	[M]Matched Samples	
Variance:	[P]Population	[S]Sample	S
Sample:	[S]Simple	[C]Cluster	S
	[T]Stratified		

Press ↑ or ↓ to move cursor.

END to Finish : ESC to Quit

Press R or S to set option
for problem attribute or press a command key.

48

** DATA INPUT **

Computerized Business Statistics
Interval Estimation - Enter Summary Data

Sample Size:	30
Mean:	44.200
Standard Deviation:	21.080

Press ↑ or ↓ to move cursor.

≡ ≡ ≡ ≡ ≡ ≡ ≡ ≡ ≡ ≡ ≡

END to Finish : ESC to Quit

Enter numeric value (>= 0)...
Command keys are not recognized when
numberic input is in progress

Computerized Business Statistics
Interval Estimation - Enter Statistics

Alpha error: 1=0.2, 2=0.1, 3=0.05, 4=0.02, 5=0.01, 6=other
Select alpha: enter 1-6 and press ←┘   3

Degrees of Freedom...................................29

Critical t (Test Statistic - alpha/2)........2.045

press ←┘

** RESULTS **

STANDARD ERROR OF THE MEAN:...................................3.8487

MEAN:...44.2000

** 95% INTERVAL ESTIMATE = 44.20 ± 7.87 **

These results show that the manager should be 95% confident that the actual rate of absenteeism
lies between 36.33 and 52.07 hours per year.

49

8.0 HYPOTHESIS TESTING

8.1 PROGRAM DESCRIPTION

This program performs hypothesis testing for one or two samples (matched or unmatched). The program can also determine the power curve with respect to Type II errors. A graphical display option is available to demonstrate the sampling distribution and decision results.

8.2 OVERVIEW

The testing of hypotheses is the process of determining whether an inference about a population is true or false. This program includes the following two testing options for both means and proportions:

◊ A **one sample** test to determine whether the sample differs significantly from the stated hypothesis.

◊ A **two sample** test to determine if they differ significantly from a population where no difference is hypothesized to exist. This test can be applied for both matched and unmatched sample data.

The following two propositions form the basis for modern hypothesis testing:

Null Hypothesis: This hypothesis often involves testing an assumption regarding the value of a population parameter. For example, one might be interested in determining whether music has a significant effect on production. In this case, production is the population parameter of interest and the null hypothesis is that music does not impact production.

Research Hypothesis: This hypothesis is usually a deduction from theory and states: "If X is true then Y should be true". For example, one can expect more production (i.e., Y) when music (i.e., X) is played than when music is not played

Associated with each null hypotheses is an alternative. The alternative is true when the null hypothesis is rejected. For example, if the null hypothesis of music having no effect on production is rejected, then the alternative hypothesis that music does indeed affect production can be accepted.

8.3 INPUT DATA

The program accepts either summary statistics or raw data. Problem data can be inputted either via terminal prompting or from a data file in the case of raw data (see Chapter 2.0). The basic input includes:

◊ Level of significance (alpha error).

◊ Population hypothesis.

◊ Sample mean.

◊ Standard deviation.

◊ Number of data points, i.e., sample size.

◊ Data values (raw data option).

8.4 MODEL OUTPUT

The following highlights the basic output from the hypothesis testing model:

◊ Standard Error.

◊ Lower Limit (if applicable).

◊ Upper Limit (if applicable).

◊ Computed Test Statistic

◊ A Conclusion to Reject or not to Reject the Stated Hypothesis.

◊ Power Curve (optional).

8.5 DEMONSTRATION EXERCISES

EXERCISE #1: The director of the Iowa Department of Motor Vehicles is interested in determining if the average customer waiting time in the new Des Moines office meets the department's guidelines. The current policy is that the average waiting time should not exceed ten minutes. The department's staff randomly sampled 30 customer waiting times over a period of one month. The results yielded a sample mean of 11.37 minutes and a sample standard deviation of 4.14 minutes. This problem consists of a single sample with a one sided upper tailed test. The null hypothesis is that $X \leq 10$. What conclusions can the director draw at a 0.05 level of significance?

Computerized Business Statistics

Hypothesis Testing - Program Options Menu

```
0.  CBS Configuration
1.  Enter Data from Keyboard
2.  Enter Data from Data Disk
3.  Enter Example Problem
4.  View Current Problem
5.  Edit current Problem
6.  Quick Reviews
7.  Run Problem
8.  Exit to Main Menu
9.  Exit to Operating System
```

press ◄— to select option under hi-lite bar
press number or up/down arrow keys to move hi-lite bar

PROGRAM PERFORMS HYPOTHESIS TESTING FOR ONE OR TWO
POPULATIONS WITH SMALL OR LARGE SAMPLES

Computerized Business Statistics

Hypothesis Testing - Set Up New Problem

Data Type:	[R]Raw	[S]Summary	S
Data Form:	[M]Means	[P]Proportions	M
Proportion data consists of values from 0 to 1.			
Population:	[1]One Population	[2]Two Populations	1
	[U]Unmatched	[M]Matched Samples	
Variance:	[P]Population	[S]Sample	S
Testing:	[1]One Sided	[2]Two Sided	1
	[L]Lower Limit	[U]Upper Limit	U
Hypothesis Value:			10

Press ↑ or ↓ to move cursor.

END to Finish : ESC to Quit

Press R or S to set option
for problem attribute or press a command key.

Computerized Business Statistics

Hypothesis Testing - Enter Summary Data

Sample Size:	30
Mean:	11.370
Standard Deviation (S):	4.140

Press ↑ or ↓ to move cursor.

Enter numeric value (>=0)...
Command keys are not recognized when numeric input is in progress.

END to Finish : ESC to Quit

Computerized Business Statistics

Interval Estimation - Enter Statistics

Alpha error: 1=0.2, 2=0.1, 3=0.05, 4=0.02, 5=0.01, 6=other

Select alpha: enter 1-6 and press ← **2**

Degrees of Freedom....................................29

Critical t (Test Statistic - alpha/2)........1.699

press ←

HYPOTHESIS TESTING

** RESULTS **

STANDARD ERROR OF MEAN: 0.7559

HYPOTHESIS VALUE:...10

UPPER LIMIT:...11.2842

MEAN:...11.3700

ALPHA ERROR:...0.0500

DEGREES OF FREEDOM:...29

CRITICAL t (TEST STATISTIC):..1.6990

COMPUTED t:..1.8125

P-VALUE:...0.0401

CONCLUSION: REJECT HYPOTHESIS

Power Curve (Y/N)? ....N
Graphic   (Y/N)?..Y

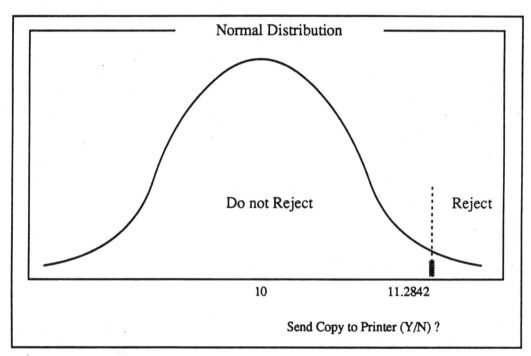

These results show that the null hypothesis indicating an average service time of ten minutes or less can be rejected at the 0.05 level of significance. This suggests that the average customer waiting time at the Des Moines office does exceed the department's guideline of 10 minutes.

EXERCISE #2: The Dietfast Company is interested in undertaking an advertising campaign to promote a newly developed diet. The company's general manager has decided to conduct a trial test program to estimate the potential effectiveness of the new diet prior to initiating the ad campaign. A random sample of eight individuals were selected to test the new diet. Each individual was weighed before and after participating in the 30 day program. The following data summarizes the results from the test program:

Participant	Weight Before	Weight After
1	149	151
2	172	167
3	216	210
4	185	178
5	137	136
6	115	112
7	155	149
8	108	106

The general manager has established a null hypothesis that the diet does not yield statistically significant results at the 0.05 level. This problem involves a matched pairs (i.e., two populations) two sided test. The null hypothesis is that U1 - U2 = 0.

** PROMPTED INPUT **

RAW (R) OR SUMMARY (S) DATA: .... R

MEANS (M) OR PROPORTIONS (P) .... M

ONE (1) OR TWO (2) POPULATIONS: 2
    UNMATHCED (U) OR MATCHED (M) .... M

POPULATION (P) OR SAMPLE (S) VARIANCE: .... S

ONE (1) OR TWO (2) SIDED TESTING: 2

HYPOTHESIS   VALUE: 0

NUMBER OF DATA POINTS: 8

NAME FOR VARIABLE #1: X1

NAME FOR VARIABLE #2: X2

** DATA INPUT **

	X1	X2
1	149	151
2	172	167
3	216	210
4	185	178
5	137	136
6	115	112
7	155	149
8	108	106

ALPHA ERROR (1=0.2, 2=0.1, 3=0.05, 4=0.02, 5=0.01, 6=Other)
    SELECT ALPHA (1-6):...3

HYPOTHESIS TESTING
** RESULTS **

STANDARD ERROR OF MEAN: 1.0856

LOWER LIMIT: ....-2.5675

HYPOTHESES VALUE:...0

UPPER LIMIT:...2.5675

MEAN OF DIFFERENCES:...3.5000

ALPHA ERROR: 0.0500

DEGREES OF FREEDOM: 7

CRITICAL t (TEST STATISTIC): 2.365

COMPUTED t:...3.2240

P-VALUE:...0.0147

CONCLUSION: REJECT HYPOTHESIS

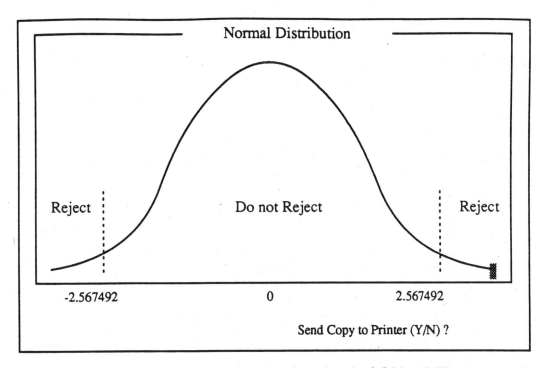

Normal Distribution

Reject ⋮ Do not Reject ⋮ Reject

-2.567492   0   2.567492

Send Copy to Printer (Y/N) ?

These results show that the null hypothesis can be rejected at the 0.05 level (The computed test statistic is greater than the critical test statistic). Therefore, the general manager can conclude that the diet does work and that the difference observed is not due to chance.

9.0 SIMPLE LINEAR CORRELATION AND REGRESSION

9.1 PROGRAM DESCRIPTION

This program computes a correlation coefficient and a linear regression equation for one dependent variable (Y) and one independent variable (X). The statistical significance of the developed model is given along with sum of the squares results. The model can be used to develop forecasts, including interval estimates, for given values of the independent variable. A graphics package is available for depicting the developed regression line and the actual data points.

9.2 OVERVIEW

The correlation coefficient (r) is an indicator of the strength of an relationship between the independent variable and the dependent variable. This statistic can vary between a +1.0 (a perfect positive relationship) to -1.0 (a perfect negative relationship. A value of r = 0 indicates that no relationship can be inferred between the two variables.

A linear regression line consists of a slope and an intercept. Together the slope and intercept form a regression equation which can be used to predict a value of Y from any value of X. The straight line is based on the relationship present in two distributions and is computed by the method of least squares. Regression models are used extensively in forecasting. For example, if a relationship can be shown to exist between an aptitude test score "X" and a level of productivity "Y", these variables can be regressed and productivity can be predicted based upon any aptitude value. Although the correlation coefficient indicates the magnitude of a relationship this should not be interpreted as a "causal" relationship. X does not cause Y; rather, the two variables tend to vary together. Thus, the aptitude test score does not cause the productivity. Rather, the degree to which variables are related is the degree to which the two distributions are measuring some common factor which underlies both.

An important extension to the correlation coefficient (r) is its square (R^2) which is called the coefficient of determination. This coefficient indicates the amount of variation in Y explained by the regression model. For example, if an r of 0.70 was obtained, the resulting R^2 of .49 means that 49% of the variation in Y is explained by the model. Typically, R^2 is the primary measure for measuring the accuracy of the developed model.

The basic assumptions underlying the development and use of the correlation coefficient and regression model are listed below:

1. The error terms are independent of each other.

2. The scatter of Y around the regression line is normally distributed.

3. The variance of Y remains constant for any value of X (i.e., Homoscedasticity)

The correlation coefficient is often used even though some of these assumptions may be violated. However, care must be exercised in interpreting the results and especially in making inferences.

9.3 DATA INPUT

Problem data can be inputted either via terminal prompting or from a data file (see Chapter 2.0). The basic input includes:

◊ Number of data points (4-200)

◊ Level of significance (alpha error)

◊ Variable names

◊ Numerical values for independent variable

◊ Numerical values for dependent variable

◊ Data file option

  • File name(s)

  • Column name(s)

  • Column number(s) for identifying dependent and independent variables

9.4 MODEL OUTPUT

The following highlights the basic output from the model:

◊ Equation Parameters
  - Intercept (Bo)
  - Slope (B1)

◊ Sum of Squares:
  - Regression
  - Error
  - Total

◊ Statistical Parameters
  - Coefficient of Determination
  - Correlation Coefficient
  - Computed t value
  - Computed p-value

◊ Statement regarding the statistical significance of b1

◊ Residual Analysis (Optional)

◊ Interval & Forecasting Analysis (Optional)

9.5 DEMONSTRATION EXERCISES

EXERCISE #1: The management at Pacific Construction Company are interested in determining the extent of the relationship between corporate advertising and sales. Pacific's vice president for marketing has collected the following data on advertising expenditures and gross sales over the past 12 months. The vice president believes that there is a simple linear relationship between advertising and sales.

Month	Advertising ($000)	Sales ($000)
Jan	$15.25	$212.18
Feb	14.15	218.27
Mar	17.35	221.45
Apr	21.05	234.56
May	19.50	241.34
Jun	16.40	225.20
Jul	12.85	203.91
Aug	9.10	212.23
Sep	14.05	198.76
Oct	18.25	212.32
Nov	19.25	214.78
Dec	14.65	222.56

Computerized Business Statistics

Simple Correlation & Regression - Program Options Menu

0.	CBS Configuration
1.	Enter Data from Keyboard
2.	Enter Data from Data Disk
3.	Enter Example Problem
4.	View Current Problem
5.	Edit current Problem
6.	Quick Reviews
7.	Run Problem
8.	Exit to Main Menu
9.	Exit to Operating System

press ◄─┘ to select option under hi-lite bar
press number or up/down arrow keys to move hi-lite bar

PROGRAM DEVELOPS A REGRESSION LINE FOR A SINGLE INDEPENDENT VARIABLE.
DATA TRANSFORMATIONS ARE AVAILABLE IN DBAS (CBS MAIN MENU ITEM #2).

** PROMPTED INPUT **

NUMBER OF DATA POINTS (4-200) ? 12

ALPHA ERROR: 1=0.2, 2=0.1, 3=0.05, 4=0.02, 5=0.01, 6=other
    SELECT ALPHA ERROR (1-6) ?.......................................3

VARIABLE NAMES:
    INDEPENDENT VARIABLE NAME ?................................ADV
    DEPENDENT VARIABLE NAME ?....................................SAL

61

** VARIABLE VALUES **

	ADV	SAL
1	15.25	212.18
2	14.15	218.27
3	17.35	221.45
4	21.05	234.56
5	19.50	241.34
6	16.40	225.20
7	12.85	203.91
8	9.10	212.23
9	14.05	198.76
10	18.25	212.32
11	19.25	214.78
12	14.65	222.56

SAVE DATA (Y/N) ? ....N

SIMPLE CORRELATION AND REGRESSION
** RESULTS **

B0 Coefficient: 183.0159
B1 Coefficient: 2.1963

Mean of X:...15.9875
Mean of Y:...218.1300
Sum of Squares Regression: 590.9362
Sum of Squares Error: 990.9610
Sum of Squares Total:...1,581.8972

Coefficient of Determination:...0.3736
Correlation Coefficient: 0.6112
Standard Error Estimate: 9.9547
Standard Error B1:...0.8994

Computed t:...2.4420
Critical t: 2.2280
p value:...0.0348

Conclusion: B1 coefficient is statistically significant.

** RESIDUAL ANALYSIS **

Number	Y-Actual	Y-Pred	Residual
1	212.1800	216.5102	-4.3302
2	218.2700	214.0942	4.1758
3	221.4500	221.1225	0.3275
4	234.5600	229.2498	5.3110
5	241.3400	225.8447	15.4953
6	225.2000	219.0360	6.1640
7	203.9100	211.2390	-7.3290
8	212.2300	203.0027	9.2273
9	198.7600	213.8746	-15.1146
10	212.3200	223.0992	-10.7792
11	214.7800	225.2956	-10.5156
12	222.5600	215.1924	7.3676

62

An analysis of these results indicates that advertising expenditures and sales are positively correlated, r = 0.61. However, the relatively low r^2 suggests that other factors may also play a role in influencing sales. Nevertheless, the developed regression equation is statistically significant (the computed t value is greater than the critical t value). The following shows the process of forecasting sales ($000) for an advertising budget of $20(000):

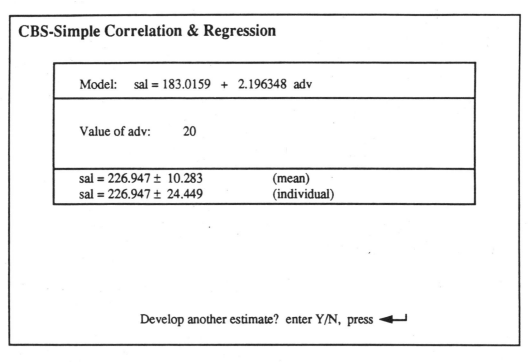

CBS-Simple Correlation & Regression

Model: sal = 183.0159 + 2.196348 adv

Value of adv: 20

sal = 226.947 ± 10.283   (mean)
sal = 226.947 ± 24.449   (individual)

Develop another estimate? enter Y/N, press ←

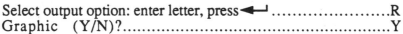

Select output option: enter letter, press ←........................R
Graphic   (Y/N)?...Y

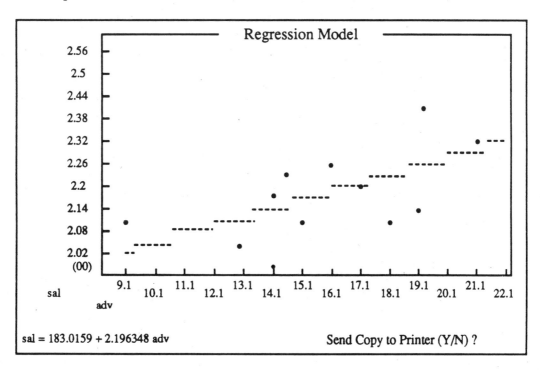

Regression Model

sal = 183.0159 + 2.196348 adv   Send Copy to Printer (Y/N) ?

EXERCISE #2: The Director of Motor Vehicles for the Los Angeles Police Department is interested in determining if a relationship exists between the age of the department's police cars and the amount spent on maintenance each year. Further, if such a relationship exists the director wishes to predict the estimated maintenance cost and develop a 95 percent confidence interval for a one year old vehicle. The following data was collected from a sample of ten cars:

AGE	COST
1	$250
1	275
2	325
2	300
3	400
4	425
4	450
5	425
5	525
6	600

** PROMPTED INPUT **

NUMBER OF DATA POINTS (4-200):.......................................10

ALPHA ERROR: 1=0.2, 2=0.1, 3=0.05, 4=0.02, 5=0.01, 6=Other
    SELECT ALPHA ERROR (1-6): 3

VARIABLE NAMES:
    INDEPENDENT VARIABLE:...AGE
    DEPENDENT VARIABLE: ....COST

VARIABLE VALUES

	AGE	COST
1	1	$250
2	1	275
3	2	325
4	2	300
5	3	400
6	4	425
7	4	450
8	5	425
9	5	525
10	6	600

SAVE DATA (Y/N):...N

SIMPLE CORRELATION AND REGRESSION
** RESULTS **

B0 Coefficient: 196.9751
B1 Coefficient: 60.7651

Mean of X: 3.3000
Mean of Y: 397.5000
Sum of Squares Regression: 103,756.4530
Sum of Squares Error: 9,306.0498
Sum of Squares Total: 113,062.5000

Coefficient of Determination: 0.9177
Correlation Coefficient: 0.9580
Standard Error Estimate: 34.1065
Standard Error B1: 6.4341

Computed t: 9.4443
Critical t: 1.8600
p-value: 0.0002

Conclusion: .... B1 coefficient is statistically significant.

An analysis of these results indicates that vehicle age and maintenance costs have a high degree of positive correlation r=.958 and that the regression equation is statistically significant. The following shows the process for forecasting maintenance costs for a one year old car:

FORECASTING

Model: Cost = ... 196.975 + 60.765 AGE

Value of AGE: 1

$$Cost = 257.74 \pm 42.231 \qquad \text{(Mean)}$$
$$Cost = 257.74 \pm 89.273 \qquad \text{(Individual)}$$

10.0 MULTIPLE REGRESSION ANALYSIS

10.1 PROGRAM DESCRIPTION

This program develops a linear regression model between a single dependent variable and multiple independent variables. The user has the option of either full or stepwise analysis. Both t-values and p-values are provided for each of the included independent variables. The model can be used to develop forecasts for the dependent variable based on given values of the independent variables. Accompanying each forecast are interval estimates for the dependent variable.

10.2 OVERVIEW

Multiple regression analysis represents a natural extension to the simple regression model. The multiple regression model is designed to incorporate more than one independent variable for estimating the dependent variable. This capability generally improves the forecast accuracy of the developed model. The basic form of the multiple regression model is given below:

$$Y = B_0 + B_1 * X_1 + B_2 * X_2 + B_3 * X_3 + B_4 * X_4 ...$$

Where Y represents the dependent variable and X_i represents the independent variables.

Multiple regression analysis generates values for the model coefficients (Bi) using the principle of least squares. The major theories of regression analysis hold that the degree to which variables are correlated is the degree to which they are measurements of something in common. Perhaps the most difficult task in multiple regression analysis is selecting the most appropriate independent variables.

Several methods are available for incorporating variables into the model. These include: full, self stepwise and auto stepwise. In the first method all of the independent variables are included in the model simultaneously. This approach ,however, suffers from the potential problem of collinearity between the independent variables. In the second method, the user specifies the order in which the variables are introduced. In the case of auto stepwise option, the first variable to be selected is the one with the highest relationship to Y. The second to be considered is the one with the next highest relationship to Y <u>and</u> the lowest to X_1. This process continues until all of the variables have been incorporated into the model or until the remaining variables are not statistically significant. The auto stepwise method is perhaps the most popular option because it limits the impact of collinearity.

Typically, a multiple regression model is evaluated using the same measures used in the simple regression model. These include the coefficient of determination, the multiple correlation coefficient, and the t values for each independent variable . Additionally, the F statistic provides an overall indicator on the significance of the developed model.

10.3 DATA INPUT

Problem data can be inputted either via terminal prompting or from a data file (see chapter 2.0). The basic input includes:

◊ Number of variables (10 max)

◊ Number of data points (200 max)

◊ Dependent variable number

◊ Level of significance (alpha error)

◊ Regression type:

- Full (all variables introduced simultaneously)
- Self stepwise (variable introduction specified by user)
- Auto stepwise (variable introduction determine by CBS)

◊ If self stepwise then order of variable introduction

◊ Variable names

◊ Variable values

◊ Data file option

- File name(s)
- Column name(s)
- Column number(s) for variables

10.4 MODEL OUTPUT

The following highlights the basic output from the multiple regression model:

◊ Intercept and variable coefficients.

◊ Standard errors for each variable coefficient.

◊ Beta values for each independent variable (Beta values provide a normalized estimate of the relative contribution of each independent variable in the regression model).

◊ Computed t values for each variable coefficient.

◊ Computed p-values for each variable coefficient (p-values report the probability that the computed variable coefficient occurred by chance).

◊ Sum of the squares.

◊ Coefficient of determination.

◊ Variable means and standard deviations (optional).

◊ Correlation matrix (optional).

◊ Residuals (optional).

◊ Computed F value (an overall measurement of the statistical significance of the model).

◊ Durbin-Watson test statistic (used to indicate the presence of auto-correlation in time series data).

Additionally, the developed model can be used for predicting values for the dependent variable (optional). The user will be prompted to provide values for each of the independent variables incorporated into the model. The developed forecast will include both a point and interval estimate for the dependent variable (Y). Two interval estimates are provided: one based on the mean value of Y and the other based on an individual value of Y.

10.5 DEMONSTRATION EXERCISES

EXERCISE #1: The Far Filtration Company manufactures filtration elements and equipment for industrial and sewage plant applications. A significant part of the company's sales revenue is generated from competitive bids. Typically, customer bid requests require specification data on filtration efficiency (measured in percent), filter strength (measured in percentage of polyester), and filter operating life (measured in months). The company's chief engineer has collected the following performance and sales data over the past 14 months. The chief engineer wishes to demonstrate to management that product quality is an important factor in sales. The chief engineer wishes to develop a stepwise multiple regression analysis to evaluate the impact of each quality factor on sales.

MONTH	Efficiency (%)	Composition (%)	Life (months)	Sales ($)
Sep	95	12.0	27	192,360
Oct	84	12.2	24	116,560
Nov	92	12.6	29	214,200
Dec	90	12.0	22	136,830
Jan	88	12.8	27	152,230
Feb	91	12.3	26	168,400
Mar	86	13.0	29	179,400
Apr	85	12.5	29	187,210
May	84	12.2	23	145,230
Jun	93	13.5	25	165,540
Jul	89	11.8	24	161,330
Aug	88	13.3	21	138,780
Sep	92	11.9	30	172,500
Oct	93	13.7	27	186,110

** PROMPTED INPUT **

RAW(R) OR CORRELATION(C) DATA: ....R

NUMBER OF VARIABLES (1-10):..4

NUMBER OF DATA POINTS ($5 \leq N \leq 200$):...............................14

VARIABLE NAMES:
    Variable 1:..EFFC
    Variable 2:..COMP
    Variable 3:..LIFE
    Variable 4:..SALE

DATA MATRIX

	EFFC	COMP	LIFE	SALE
1	95	12.0	27	192,360
2	84	12.2	24	116,560
3	92	12.6	29	214,200
4	90	12.0	22	136,830
5	88	12.8	27	152,230
6	91	12.3	26	168,400
7	86	13.0	29	179,400
8	85	12.5	29	187,210
9	84	12.2	23	145,230
10	93	13.5	25	165,540
11	89	11.8	24	161,330
12	88	13.3	21	138,780
13	92	11.9	30	172,500
14	93	13.7	27	186,110

DEPENDENT VARIABLE NUMBER (1-4) ? 4

REGRESSION TYPE:
   F = FULL
   S = SELF STEPWISE
   A = AUTO STEPWISE
      SELECT OPTION (F,S,A) ?...A

ALPHA ERROR 1=0.2, 2=0.1, 3=0.05, 4=0.025, 5=0.02, 6=0.01, 7=Other
      SELECT ALPHA (1-7) ?..3

SAVE DATA (Y/N) ? ....N

MULTIPLE VARIABLE REGRESSION

** Results - Iteration 1 **

Variable	B-coeff	std err	Beta	t value	p-value
LIFE	6.9607	1.7122	0.7611	4.0654	0.0016

B0 Intercept:...-15.0041
Critical t: 2.1790

Sum Squares Regression:..5,083.9419
Sum Squares Error:..3,691.3240
Sum Squares Total:..8,775.2656

Mean Square Regression:..5,083.9419
Mean Square Residual:...307.6103

C.O.D. (R-Squared):...0.5793
Adjusted C.O.D. (R-Squared):...0.5443
Multiple Correlation Coefficient:.....................................0.7611
Standard Error Estimate:..17.5388

dOf Regression:..1
dOf Error:...12

Critical F:..4.7500
Computed F:...16.5272
F(p-value):..0.0011

** Iteration 2 **

Variable	B-coeff	std err	Beta	t value	p-value
LIFE	6.1510	1.5236	0.6726	4.0372	0.0020
EFFC	2.7158	1.2082	0.3745	2.2478	0.0461

B0 Intercept:...-236.4873
Critical t:..2.2010

Sum Squares Regression:..6,245.7729
Sum Squares Error:..2,529.4924
Sum Squares Total:..8,775.2656

Mean Square Regression:..3,122.8865
Mean Square Residual:...229.9539

C.O.D. (R-Squared):...0.7117
Adjusted C.O.D. (R-Squared):...0.6593
Multiple Correlation Coefficient:.....................................0.8437
Standard Error Estimate:..15.1642

dOf Regression:..2
dOf Error:...11

Critical F:..3.9800
Computed F:...13.5805
F(p-value):..0.0010
Durbin-Watson Statistic:...2.5440

** ** REMAINING VARIABLES ARE INSIGNIFICANT **

71

** RESIDUAL ANALYSIS **

Number	Y-Actual	Y-Pred	Residual
1	192.3600	187.5861	4.7739
2	116.5600	139.2598	-22.6998
3	114.2000	191.7407	22.4593
4	136.8300	143.2524	-6.4224
5	152.2300	168.5758	-16.3458
6	168.4000	170.5721	-2.1721
7	179.4000	175.4462	3.9538
8	187.2100	172.7304	14.4796
9	145.2300	133.1088	12.1212
10	165.5400	169.8526	-4.3126
11	161.3300	152.8386	8.4914
12	138.7800	131.6699	7.1101
13	172.5000	197.8917	-25.3917
14	186.1100	182.1546	3.9554

CORRELATION MATRIX				
	EFFC	**COMP**	**LIFE**	**SALE**
EFFC	1	0.1242	0.2364	0.5335
COMP		1	0.0157	0.1490
LIFE			1	0.7611
SALE				1

Variable	Mean Value	Standard Deviation
EFFC	89.286	3.583
COMP	12.557	0.617
LIFE	25.929	2.841
SALE	165.477	25.981

These results show that both filter life and efficiency appear to be positively correlated with company sales. The developed model explains approximately 71% of the variability in sales (i.e., $r^2 = 0.7117$).

EXERCISE #2: The management at Offshore Realty is interested in determining the extent of any relationship between selling price and location(measured on a 1 to 5 scale), lot size (FT^2) and number of bedrooms. A survey of 50 recently sold homes yielded the following correlation matrix along with means and standard deviations for the four variables. Management wishes to use a full regression for this analysis.

CORRELATION MATRIX				
	Location	Lot Size	# Bedrooms	Price
Location	1			
Lot Size	0.3	1		
# Bedrooms	0.1	0.6	1	
Price	0.8	0.7	0.5	1

** MEANS & STANDARD DEVIATIONS **

	Location	Lot Size	# Bedrooms	Price
Means	3	8000	3	150000
S.D.	1	2000	1	20000

** PROMPTED INPUT **

RAW(R) OR CORRELATION(C) DATA: C

NUMBER OF VARIABLES (2-10):...4

NUMBER OF DATA POINTS (7-200):....................................50

VARIABLE NAMES:
#1:..LOC
#2:..LOT
#3:..BED
#4:..SEL

CORRELATION COEFFICIENT MATRIX				
	LOC	LOT	BED	SEL
LOC	1	0.3	0.1	0.8
LOT		1	0.6	0.7
BED			1	0.5
SEL				1

MEANS & STANDARD DEVIATIONS

Variable	Mean Value	Standard Deviation
LOC	3	1
LOT	8000	2000
BED	3	1
SEL	150000	20000

DEPENDENT VARIABLE NUMBER(1-4) ?..............................4

REGRESSION TYPE:
   F = FULL
   S = SELF STEPWISE
   A = AUTO STEPWISE
      SELECT OPTION (F,S,A) ?...F

ALPHA ERROR 1=0.2 ,2=0.1, 3=0.05, 4=0.025, 5=0.02, 6=0.01, 7=other
      SELECT ALPHA (1-7) ?..3

SAVE DATA (Y/N) ? ....N

MULTIPLE VARIABLE REGRESSION
** RESULTS **

Variable	B-coeff	std err	Beta	t value	p-value
LOC	13,333.3340	982.9462	0.6667	13.5647	0
LOT	3.7500	0.6113	0.3750	6.1348	0
BED	4,166.6665	1,172.0888	0.2083	3.5549	0

B0 Intercept:..67,500
Critical t: 2.0147

Sum Squares Regression:...17,639,999,000
Sum Squares Error:..1,959,999,490
Sum Squares Total:...19,599,999,000

Mean Square Regression:..5,880,000,000
Mean Square Residual:...42,608,684

C.O.D. (R-Squared):...0.9000
Adjusted C.O.D. (R-Squared):...0.8935
Multiple Correlation Coefficient:..0.9487
Standard Error Estimate: 6,527.5327

dOf Regression:..3
dOf Error:..46

Critical F: 2.8160
Computed F:...138
F(p-value):...0.0001

An analysis of these results shows that all three independent variables are statistically significant at the 0.05 level and that the overall relationship is statistically significant. The full model is:

$$SEL = 67500 + 13333.33*LOC + 3.75*LOT + 4166.66*BED$$

This model can be used for estimating housing prices for given values of the independent variables. The following CBS output illustrates the forecasting process for a home with a location rating of 4, a lot size of 10,000 FT^2 and four bedrooms. The forecast reveals a point estimate of $175,000 with a 5% interval width of $3,174 (mean).

** FORECASTING **

Variable	B-coeff	Significant	Value
LOC	13,333.33	yes	4
LOT	3.75	yes	10000
BED	4,166.66	yes	4

SEL = 175000 ± 3174 (MEAN)

SEL = 175000 ± 13528 (INDIVIDUAL)

11.0 TIME SERIES AND FORECASTING

11.1 PROGRAM DESCRIPTION

This program analyzes time series data using least squares, moving averages, and exponential smoothing techniques. The program can also analyze seasonal data. A graphics option is available which depicts the raw data and trend results as a function of time.

11.2 OVERVIEW

Times series analysis, as the name suggests, is used to evaluate historical data patterns. A time series can be defined as a sequence of data values recorded over time. Most organizations maintain extensive time series data bases on a variety of financial and other performance measures. Generally, time series analysis consists of decomposing the data into a number of component parts as a basis for determining specific patterns of behavior. The usual approach is to divide the time series into the following four components: long term trend(T), cyclic(C) variation, seasonal(S) variation, and irregular(I) variation.

Typically, a detailed analysis of these time series building blocks provides the basis for making predictions regarding future events. This prediction process is called forecasting. There exits a wide range of forecasting techniques. Experience indicates that no one forecasting method is appropriate for all situations. Presented in following is a brief summary of the more popular methods used for analyzing time series data and for developing forecasts:

◊ **Least Squares:**   Uses time along with other independent variables to predict values for the dependent variable. Autoregressive analysis is a special form where one or more of the independent variables represent historical values of the dependent variables, i.e., lagged values.

◊ **Moving Averages:**   A process that averages overlapping groups of data based on a specific number of periods. Typically, two types of averages are used: simple and weighted. In the former case, each of the data points are treated with equal emphasis while in the latter case more emphasis is placed on the latest data values in the average.

◊ **Exponential Smoothing:**   A process that forecasts the next period based on the difference between the previous forecast and actual value. Exponential smoothing is one of the most popular forecasting methods due, in part, to its accuracy and ease of use. Typically, three types of exponential models are used: simple smoothing, smoothing with trend and smoothing with trend and seasonal. Each of these models require one or more smoothing coefficients. In some cases, these coefficients can be optimized based on minimizing the errors associated with the developed forecasts.

◊ **Seasonal Indexes:**   In many cases, a time series is influenced by the presence of seasonal effects. A seasonal effect is defined as a repeating pattern that occurs within the period of a year. Seasonal effects can mask the presence of trends in the time series and therefore need to be removed prior to developing a forecast. The normal process used to "deseasonalize" a time series is to compute a set of seasonal indexes.

76

11.3 DATA INPUT

Problem data can be input either via terminal prompting or from a data file (see chapter 2.0). The basic input data includes:

◊ Forecasting Method:

- Least Squares (regression)
- Moving Averages (simple & weighted)
- Simple Exponential Smoothing
- Exponential Smoothing with Trend Factoring
- Exponential Smoothing with Trend and Seasonal Factoring
- Seasonal Indexes

◊ Number of Data Points (4-200)

◊ Data Values

◊ Smoothing Constants (exponential time series)

◊ Data File Option

- File name(s)
- Column name(s)
- Column number for variables of interest

For the seasonal option, a three period moving average is used to estimate the base trend line.

11.4 MODEL OUTPUT

The following highlights the basic output from this model:

◊ Mean Square Error (MSE) and Mean Absolute Deviation (MAD).

◊ Forecast.

◊ Actual versus predicted values by period.

The program can determine the optimal values for the number of periods in the moving average (option #2) or the smoothing coefficients (options #3-#5) based on either the MSE or MAD errors.

11.5 DEMONSTRATION EXERCISES

EXERCISE #1: Dialnet Telephone Exchange is a regional communications company serving the southwestern United States. The firm's general manager is interested in preparing a forecast of new phone installations for the coming year. The general manager has collected the following phone installation data (000) for the past 11 years.

Year	Installations (000)
1976	45.5
1977	79.2
1978	77.8
1979	81.4
1980	102.2
1981	124.8
1982	132.6
1983	156.3
1984	161.2
1985	168.6
1986	174.2

The general manager wishes to developed a forecast for the next period using a three period moving average.

** PROMPTED INPUT **

OPTIONS   1 = LEAST SQUARES
                2 = MOVING AVERAGES
                3 = SIMPLE EXPONENTIAL SMOOTHING
                4 = SMOOTHING WITH TREND FACTORING
                5 = TREND AND SEASONAL SMOOTHING
                6 = SEASONAL INDICES

SELECT OPTION (1-6): 2

SIMPLE OR WEIGHTED (S/W):...................................S

NUMBER OF DATA POINTS (4-200):....................................11

NUMBER OF PERIODS IN AVERAGE (2-12): 3

VARIABLE NAME:..INST

** DATA INPUT **

INST

1	45.5
2	79.2
3	77.8
4	81.4
5	102.2
6	124.8
7	132.6
8	156.3
9	161.2
10	168.6
11	174.2

SAVE DATA (Y/N) ? ....N

TIME SERIES AND FORECASTING
** RESULTS **

Model Type:..Moving Averages - Simple
Number of Periods in Average:...3
Number of Periods:..11

Average INST:...118.5273
Mean Square Error:..672.4824
Mean Absolute Deviation:..24.3208
Forecast for Period 12:...168

** RESIDUAL ANALYSIS **

Period	INST (Yp)	Calculated (Sp-1)	Residual (Yp - Sp-1)
1	45.5000	45.5000	0
2	79.2000	79.2000	0
3	77.8000	77.8000	0
4	81.4000	67.5000	13.9000
5	102.2000	79.4667	22.7333
6	124.8000	87.1333	37.6667
7	132.6000	102.8000	29.8000
8	156.3000	119.8667	36.4333
9	161.2000	137.9000	23.3000
10	168.6000	150.0333	18.5667
11	174.2000	162.0333	12.1667

#1A. Optimize number of periods in average for MSE (select #1)

RESULTS
** OPTIMIZED FOR MSE **

Period	INST (Yp)	Calculated (Sp-1)	Residual (Yp - Sp-1)
1	45.5000	45.5000	0
2	79.2000	45.5000	33.7000
3	77.8000	79.2000	-1.4000
4	81.4000	77.8000	3.6000
5	102.2000	81.4667	20.8000
6	124.8000	102.2000	22
7	132.6000	124.2000	0.6000
8	156.3000	124.8000	7.8000
9	161.2000	132.6000	23.7000
10	168.6000	156.3000	4.9000
11	174.2000	161.2000	13

#1B. Optimize number of periods in average for MAD (select #2)

RESULTS
** OPTIMIZED FOR MAD **

Model Type: ....Moving Averages - Simple
Number of Periods in Average: 3
Number of Periods 11

Optimized Number of Periods in Average: 1
Average INST: 118.5273
Mean Square Error: 282.6670
Mean Average Deviation: 13.500
Forecast for Period 12: 174.2000

RESIDUAL ANALYSIS - OPTIMIZED FOR MAD

Period	INST (Yp)	Calculated (Sp-1)	Residual (Yp - Sp-1)
1	45.5000	45.5000	0
2	79.2000	45.5000	33.7000
3	77.8000	79.2000	-1.4000
4	81.4000	77.8000	3.6000
5	102.2000	81.4000	20.8000
6	124.8000	102.2000	22.6000
7	132.6000	124.2000	7.8000
8	156.3000	124.8000	23.7000
9	161.2000	132.6000	4.9000
10	168.6000	156.3000	7.4000
11	174.2000	161.2000	5.6000

To generate the graph below, first chose 'R = Return to Time Series...' then respond 'Y' to the the graphics prompt.

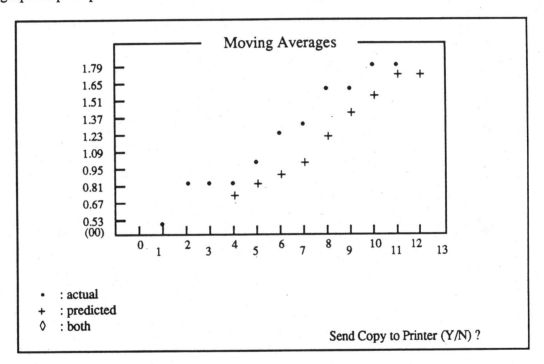

These results show a forecast of 168(000) installations for 1987. This forecast was based on a three period moving average. The manager may wish to change the number of periods used in the calculations or to use one of the other forecasting methods as a means for evaluating the present estimate.

EXERCISE #2: Another concern of the general manager at Dialnet Telephone Exchange is the potential variation in sales over the year. More specifically, the general manager is interested in estimating seasonal quarterly indices for sales. The general manager has collected the following quarterly sales data between 1977 and 1983.

Quarterly Sales
($ millions)

Year	1st	2nd	3rd	4th
1977	10.3	12.8	8.2	9.8
1978	10.0	13.4	7.5	10.3
1979	11.1	16.3	7.7	9.5
1980	15.9	20.4	9.9	11.2
1981	18.4	22.8	14.8	14.8
1982	19.7	23.1	15.4	14.5
1983	22.2	24.3	16.5	15.4

SAVE DATA (Y/N) ? ....N

** PROMPTED INPUT **

OPTIONS
    1 = LEAST SQUARES
    2 = MOVING AVERAGES
    3 = SIMPLE EXPONENTIAL SMOOTHING
    4 = SMOOTHING WITH TREND FACTORING
    5 = TREND AND SEASONAL SMOOTHING
    6 = SEASONAL INDICES

SELECT OPTION (1-6) ? 6

NUMBER OF YEARS (2-10) ? 7

VARIABLE NAME ? ....SALES

TIME SERIES AND FORECASTING

** RESULTS **

Model Type:...Classical Seasonal Indices
Number of Periods:...28

SEASONAL INDICES

Period	Quarter	Value	Trend	S-I
1	1	10.3000	-	-
	2	12.8000	-	-
	3	8.2000	10.2375	0.8010
	4	9.8000	10.2750	0.9538
2	1	10.0000	10.2625	0.9744
	2	13.4000	10.2375	1.3089
	3	7.5000	10.4375	0.7186
	4	10.3000	10.9375	0.9417
3	1	11.1000	11.3250	0.9801
	2	16.3000	11.2500	1.4489
	3	7.7000	11.7500	0.6553
	4	9.5000	12.8625	0.7386

Period	Quarter	Value	Trend	S-I
4	1	15.9000	13.6500	1.1648
	2	20.4000	14.1375	1.4430
	3	9.9000	14.6625	0.6752
	4	11.2000	15.2750	0.7332
5	1	18.4000	16.1875	1.1367
	2	22.8000	17.2500	1.3217
	3	14.8000	17.8625	0.8286
	4	14.8000	18.0625	0.8194
6	1	19.7000	18.1750	1.0839
	2	23.1000	18.2125	1.2684
	3	15.4000	18.4875	0.8330
	4	14.5000	18.9500	0.7652
7	1	22.2000	19.2375	1.1540
	2	24.3000	19.4875	1.2470
	3	16.5000	-	-
	4	15.4000	-	-

SEASONAL INDEX BY QUARTER

Quarter	Average SI Component	Seasonal Index
1	1.0823	1.0850
2	1.3396	1.3430
3	0.7519	0.7538
4	0.8253	0.8274

These results show a considerable swing in sales levels between the second quarter and the third and fourth quarters. The computed seasonal indexes can be used by the general manager for "deseasonalizing" the raw sales data as a means for discovering the presence of any trends.

12.0 CHI-SQUARE ANALYSIS

12.1 PROGRAM DESCRIPTION

This program performs chi-square analysis hypothesis testing for both goodness-of-fit and independence. A graphical display option is available to demonstrate the chi-square distribution.

12.2 OVERVIEW

The chi-square statistic is one of the most frequently used analytical tools in business. It is predominantly used to determine if relationships exist between variables when the data is in frequency form. Most market studies, segmentation studies and questionnaires are analyzed using the chi-square statistic. The two basic applications of the chi-square statistic are as follows:

1. To test whether a set of observed frequencies departs from a set of expected frequencies. This test procedure, called the "goodness-of-fit," is often used to determine if the observed frequency data matches one of the classical probability distributions (e.g., normal).

2. To test whether two variables appear to be related as measured by frequency data. This test procedure, called the "test of independence," is performed using a contingency table.

The null hypothesis for these two model options are:

Goodness-of-fit: The expected departure of data observations from expected values is zero. If the computed chi-square statistic is larger than the critical value then the null hypothesis of no difference can be rejected.

Test of Independence: Two variables are independent (unrelated) in the population. If the computed chi-square statistic is greater than the critical value then the null hypothesis that these two variables are unrelated can be rejected. Rejection of the null hypothesis supports an inference of a relationship between the two variables in the population.

This program also generates p-values for each problem application. A p-value indicates the chance that the observed results occurred by chance. The basic assumptions underlying the use of this "nonparametric" statistic are the following:

1. The data is in frequency form.

2. Each cell of the contingency table is mutually exclusive and independent.

3. The expected frequency for any cell is adequate in size (5 or more).

4. The nature of the population distribution is unknown.

12.3 DATA INPUT

Problem data can be inputted either via terminal prompting or from a data file (see Chapter 2.0). The basic input includes:

◊ Level of Significance (i.e., alpha error).

◊ Number of Observations.

◊ Labels.

◊ Observations.

◊ Expected Values (for goodness-of-fit).

◊ Data File Option:

- File name.

- Labels(s).

- Column number(s) for identity observations and expected values.

12.4 MODEL OUTPUT

◊ Computed chi-square statistic.

◊ Computed p-value.

◊ Statement regarding hypothesis (i.e., reject or do not reject).

12.5 DEMONSTRATION EXERCISES

EXERCISE #1: The Clearwater Bottling Company is interested in converting from glass containers to plastic containers. Prior to initiating this change, Clearwater's management wished to determine the public's reaction to the new containers. The company's marketing department conducted a ten week survey to measure the impact of the proposed change on sales. The survey consisted of monitoring sales in ten stores of similar size. Five of the stores were to continue to stock glass bottles while THE OTHER FIVE WOULD STOCK THE NEW PLAXTIC BOTTLES. The following data summarizes the results from the survey:

BOTTLES SOLD

Weeks	Glass	Plastic
1	520	470
2	490	500
3	510	505
4	515	515
5	495	505
6	525	510
7	500	505
8	515	510
9	495	515
10	505	500

The companies management would like to know if there was significant difference in sales between the two types of containers. One approach for evaluating this problem is to utilize a Chi-Square analysis. In this case, the collected data can be classified into several groups. Perhaps the simplest approach is to partition the data into two categories based on the average of the baseline, i.e., glass bottles. This process results in four observations above the mean and six observations below the mean. In contrast, the expected values for the two categories is five.

** PROMPTED INPUT **

GOODNESS OF FIT (1)
TEST FOR INDEPENDENCE (2)
    SELECT OPTION (1-2):...1

NUMBER OF ROWS (2-10):...2

ALPHA ERROR: 1=0.1, 2=0.05, 3=0.02, 4=0.01, 5=Other
    SELECT ALPHA (1-5):..2

** DATA INPUT **

	OBSERVED	EXPECTED
1	4	5
2	6	5

CHI-SQUARE ANALYSIS

** RESULTS **

CRITICAL CHI-SQUARE:..3.8415

COMPUTED   CHI-SQUARE:..0.4000

P-VALUE:..0.4531

CONCLUSION: ....DO NOT REJECT NULL

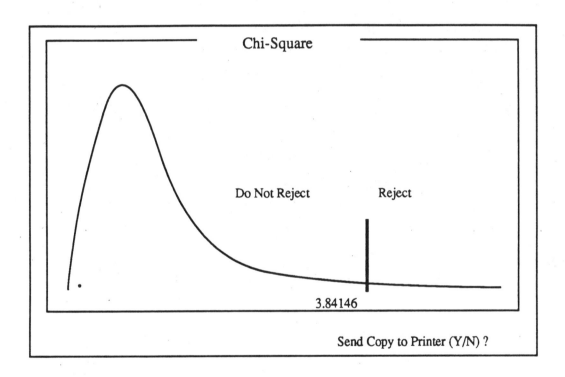

These results suggest that sales for bottle water should not be affected by switching to the plastic containers. More specifically, the computed chi-square value is less than the critical chi-square value which sustains the null hypothesis of no difference (i.e., do not reject Ho).

87

EXERCISE #2: A sport preference poll shows the following count data for the three most popular professional sports in the U.S. by men and women. What conclusions can be drawn regarding the preference for sports by sex at the 0.05 level?

FAVORITE SPORT

SEX	Baseball	Basketball	Football
Men	19	5	24
Women	16	18	16

** PROMPTED INPUT **

GOODNESS OF FIT (1)
TEST FOR INDEPENDENCE (2)
    SELECT OPTION (1-2):..2

NUMBER OF COLUMNS (2-10):..3

NUMBER OF ROWS (2-10):...2

ALPHA ERROR: 1=0.1, 2=0.05, 3=0.02, 4=0.01, 5=Other
    SELECT ALPHA (1-5):..2

COLUMN NAMES:
    COLUMN 1:...BASE
    COLUMN 2:...BASK
    COLUMN 3:...FOOT

** DATA INPUT **

	BASE	BASK	FOOT
ROW # 1	19	15	24
ROW # 2	16	18	16

88

CHI-SQUARE ANALYSIS

** OBSERVATIONS **

ROWS	BASE	BASK	FOOT	TOTAL
1	19	15	24	58
2	16	18	16	50
Total	35	33	40	108

** EXPECTED VALUES **

ROWS	BASE	BASK	FOOT	TOTAL
1	18.796	17.722	21.481	58
2	16.204	15.278	18.519	50
Total	33	33	40	108

** RESULTS **

CRITICAL CHI-SQUARE:..5.9915

COMPUTED   CHI-SQUARE:...1.5458

P-VALUE:...0.4481

CONCLUSION: DO NOT REJECT NULL

The results from this analysis show that men and women show a similar preference for the three major professional sports.

13.0 ANALYSIS OF VARIANCE

13.1 PROGRAM DESCRIPTION

This program performs analysis of variance for one to two variables (factors) with two to five population groups per variable. The primary objective is to determine if the means of the multiple populations are equal. The two-way model permits analysis of both block and two-factor data.

13.2 OVERVIEW

Analysis of variance (ANOVA) is a primary tool for statistical research and analysis. As in the case with bi-variate and multi-variate models, ANOVA attempts to segregate the total variance into two parts: explained and unexplained. Analysis of variance represents a logical extension of hypothesis testing for two populations. ANOVA is designed to test whether more than two populations are equal. ANOVA is interpreted by the standard F statistic. The requirements for its use tend to be more stringent than in the case of multiple regression. However, when the application has many groups means to compare, or when it is desired to determine the presence of "interactive" effects, the use of ANOVA is more appropriate. Typically, interactive effects occur when two or more independent variables operate together on the dependent variable. For the ANOVA model each independent variable is called a factor.

In principle, the generalized ANOVA model can be used to analyze any number of factors and any number of groupings within each factor. In most business applications, however, the number of factors is usually restricted to a maximum of two and the number of groupings to a maximum of five. Typically, ANOVA problems with more than two factors are analyzed using multiple regression. Furthermore, the two-factor model can analyze either a block or a two independent variable design. The block design is limited to a total of five observations per group.

Basically, there are two type of factors that can be analyzed using the ANOVA model: fixed effects and random effects. The fixed effects model is one where only specific values of the independent variables are of interest. In the random effects case, the factors represent only a sample of the populations levels of interest. The ANOVA models presented in this program are designed to solve the fixed effects option. However, for the one factor case the computational procedure for both options is identical.

A pairwise comparison (Tukey Test) is used to identify which means differ from the rest when the levels of a factor are shown to be statistically different. This test procedure requires inputting the test statistic for a given level of significance and degrees of freedom. This test value can be obtained from the table given in appendix F. The printout reports which set of means are significantly different.

13.3 DATA INPUT

Problem data can be inputted either via terminal prompting or from a data file (See Chapter 2.0). The basic input includes:

◊ Number of independent variables or factors (1-2).

   • The two factor design offers the selection of Block (B) or Two Variables (T)

◊ Number of groups (2-5).

◊ Level of significance (alpha error).

◊ Number of data points per cell.

◊ Variable values for each cell.

In the case of the two independent variable model, the rows represent the first factor and the columns the second factor. Additionally, the type of analysis (i.e., block or two-factor) must be identified.

13.4 MODEL OUTPUT

The following highlights the basic output from the ANOVA model:

◊ Sum of squares by effect.

◊ Mean squares by effect.

◊ F statistics by effect.

◊ A conclusion regarding the null hypothesis (i.e., to reject or not reject) by effect.

◊ A pairwise comparison (i.e., Tukey Test) identifies the significant groups when the null hypothesis is rejected.

13.5 DEMONSTRATION EXERCISES

EXERCISE #1: The production manager at the Mable Cable Company is interested in determining the impact of part-time employees on production output. Traditionally, the company has used part-timers during periods of peak demand. However, the production manager is concerned that the actual level of production may drop if the mix of part-timers to full-timers becomes too high. The production manager has decided to conduct a 10 day test using the following three levels of part-timers: low (less than 10%), medium (10-30%), and high (above 30%). The following table presents production data and group means from the 10 day sample:

PRODUCTION LEVEL

High	Medium	Low
0.659	0.911	1.230
0.330	1.010	1.490
0.680	1.000	0.998
0.820	0.898	1.010
0.626	0.992	1.230
0.831	1.110	1.110
0.595	0.900	1.440
0.439	0.998	1.000
0.649	1.010	1.150
0.800	0.944	1.960

The production manager plans to use the one-way ANOVA procedure to test at the 0.05 level if production levels are influenced by the proportion of part-timers.

** PROMPTED INPUT **

NUMBER OF VARIABLES (1-2): 1

NUMBER OF GROUPS (2-5):...3

ALPHA ERROR:...0.05

NUMBER OF DATA POINTS PER GROUP:
    COLUMN 1:...10
    COLUMN 2:...10
    COLUMN 3:...10

COLUMN NAMES:
    COLUMN 1:..HIGH
    COLUMN 2:..MED
    COLUMN 3:..LOW

** DATA INPUT **

HIGH	MED	LOW
0.659	0.911	1.230
0.330	1.010	1.490
0.680	1.000	0.998
0.820	0.898	1.010
0.626	0.992	1.230
0.831	1.110	1.110
0.595	0.900	1.440
0.439	0.998	1.000
0.649	1.010	1.150
0.800	0.944	1.960

SAVE DATA (Y/N) ? ....N

ANALYSIS OF VARIANCE

** RESULTS **

Source of Variance	Sum of Squares	Degrees of Freedom	Mean Square	Computed F-Value
Columns	1.919	2	0.960	23.898
Error	1.084	27	0.040	
Totals	3.004	29		

CRITICAL F (COL) :   3.35   * REJECT NULL HYPOTHESIS *

The null hypothesis of no difference in production can be rejected because the computed F of 23.898 is larger than the critical F of 3.35 That is, the production manager can conclude that the percentage of part-timers does impact the level of production.

PERFORM PAIRWISE TEST Y/N?......................................Y

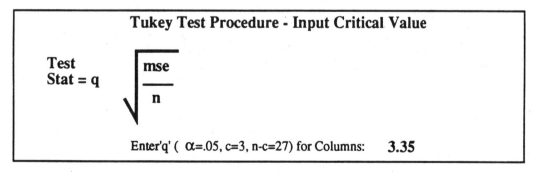

Tukey Test Procedure - Input Critical Value

$$\text{Test Stat} = q \sqrt{\frac{mse}{n}}$$

Enter 'q' (α=.05, c=3, n-c=27) for Columns: **3.35**

Tukey's Pairwise Comparison

	MEAN	MEAN	DIFF	CRITERIA
		Column Effects		
C1-C2:	0.643	0.977 =	0.334 >	.......0.224
C1-C3:	0.643	1.262 =	0.619 >	.......0.224
C2-C3:	0.977	1.262 =	0.285 >	.......0.224

EXERCISE #2: The personnel director at Johnson Carbide wishes to study employee productivity. More specifically, the director is interested in determining whether productivity is related to the management style of the company's first line supervisors and plant location. The director has the following production data as a function of plant location and leadership style over a two week period:

PLANT LOCATION

LEADERSHIP TYPE	West	Midwest	East
Autocratic	205	275	315
	225	195	254
Democratic	390	350	313
	365	345	304

The null hypothesis is that neither leadership type, plant location or the combination of both have an impact on production. The director wishes to test this hypothesis at a 5% percent level of significant.

** PROMPTED INPUT **

NUMBER OF VARIABLES (1-2): 2

BLOCK OR TWO-FACTOR ANALYSIS (B/T): ....T

VARIABLE #1 NUMBER OF GROUPS (2-5):............................2
VARIABLE #2 NUMBER OF GROUPS (2-5):............................3

ALPHA ERROR (0-1): 0.05

NUMBER OF DATA POINTS PER GROUP:

	COLUMN 1	COLUMN 2	COLUMN 3
ROW 1	2	2	2
ROW 2	2	2	2

COLUMN NAMES:

	COLUMN 1	COLUMN 2	COLUMN 3
ROW 1	EAST	MIDW	WEST
ROW 2	EAST	MIDW	WEST

** DATA INPUT **

	EAST	MIDW	WEST
ROW #1	205	275	315
	225	195	254
ROW #2	390	350	313
	365	345	304

SAVE DATA (Y/N)? ....N

ANALYSIS OF VARIANCE

** RESULTS **

Source of Variance	Sum of Squares	Degrees of Freedom	Mean Square	Computed F-Value
ROWS	29800.334	1	29800.334	31.781
COLUMNS	70.167	2	35.083	0.037
INTER	9838.167	2	4919.084	5.246
ERROR	5626	6	937.667	
TOTALS	45334.668	11		

CRITICAL F (ROW) :......................................5.99   REJECT NULL
CRITICAL F (INT) :.......................................5.14   REJECT NULL
CRITICAL F (COL) :......................................5.14   DO NOT REJECT NULL

The above table presents the analysis of variance results. Notice that the table contains a total of five sources instead of the three in the previous exercise. The two additional sources represent the second variable and the interactive effects between the two variables. These results show that both age and educational level are statistically significant. The computed F for leadership style (row variable) is 31.781 compared to the critical F of 5.99. This result suggests production output is dependent on leadership style. However, the effects of the column variable (plant location) on production is not statistically significant since the computed F is less than the critical F. On the other hand, the interactive effect which combines both leadership style and plant location is statistically significant. This suggests that the impact of leadership style on production varies by plant location.

EXERCISE #3: The Secretary of the Department of Education wishes to determine what effects different amounts of exercise have on test scores in primary school-aged children. In addition, she wants to see if the overall size of the school has any bearing on test scores. The following data shows the average test scores of four second-grade classes, taken from five different size schools.

SCHOOL SIZE

DURATION OF EXERCISE	3,500 (class 1)	2,500 (class 2)	1,500 (class 3)	500 (class 4)
20 min	87.6	74.5	83.5	90.4
30 min	79.8	68.5	90.3	93.2
40 min	85.2	79.0	89.4	88.8
50 min	83.4	80.6	86.7	87.2
1 hour	89.0	77.9	84.2	89.1

The null hypothesis is that neither the duration of exercise, school size, nor the combination of both have an impact on test scores. The Secretary wishes to test this hypothesis at a 5% percent level of significant.

** PROMPTED INPUT **

NUMBER OF VARIABLES (1-2): 2

VARIABLE #1 NUMBER OF GROUPS (2-5):............................5
VARIABLE #2 NUMBER OF GROUPS (2-5):............................4

BLOCK OR TWO-FACTOR ANALYSIS (B/T): ....B

ALPHA ERROR (0-1): 0.05

** DATA INPUT **

	3,500	2,500	1,500	500
ROW 1	87.6	74.5	83.5	90.4
ROW 2	79.8	68.5	90.3	93.2
ROW 3	85.2	79.0	89.4	88.8
ROW 4	83.4	80.6	86.7	87.2
ROW 5	89.0	77.9	84.2	89.1

SAVE DATA (Y/N)?..N

ANALYSIS OF VARIANCE

** RESULTS **

Source of Variance	Sum of Squares	Degrees of Freedom	Mean Square	Computed F-Value
BLOCKS	16.518	4	4.129	0.268
COLUMNS	518.105	3	172.702	11.207
ERROR	184.921	12	15.410	
TOTALS	719.545	19		

CRITICAL F (BLK) : 3.26..........................DO NOT REJECT NULL
CRITICAL F (COL) : 3.49.......................REJECT NULL HYPOTHESIS

97

14.0 NONPARAMETRIC METHODS

14.1 PROGRAM DESCRIPTION

This program determines the statistical significance of sample data drawn from population(s) whose distribution is unknown or where the data is ranked or ordered into categories. This program contains five of the more commonly used nonparametric methods : Wilcoxon Rank-Sum Test, Runs Test, Wilcoxon Signed-Rank Test, Spearman Rank Correlation, and Kruskal-Wallis Test.

14.2 OVERVIEW

Most of the previously presented statistical methods required an assumption that the samples be greater than or equal to 30 ($n \geq 30$), and that they are drawn from a normal population. When such an assumption is untenable the usual approach is to employ nonparametric analysis. These statistical techniques are called nonparametric because they make no assumptions about the population shape, or parameter, from which the samples are drawn. More specifically, nonparametric statistical methods should be used in the following instances:

◊ When the sample size is small and the population distribution is unknown.

◊ When the data is in either rank or categorical form.

Presented in the following are brief summaries of the nonparametric models contained in the program:

1. Wilcoxon Rank-Sum Test: (Mann-Whitney)

This test procedure is used to determine if two independent samples were drawn from identical populations. The computational process involves combining and ranking the data from the two samples and then analyzing the resultant ranks in the original groups. The null hypothesis for this test is that the two populations are identical.

2. Runs Test:

This test procedure is used to determine if the samples are random. A run is a succession of identical characters. The presence of too few or too many runs may indicate the presence of a trend or a non-random sample. The two input data options are:

• **Raw:** The input consists of the actual measurements, which are then processed into a series of +1s and -1s based on the median.
• **Processed:** The input consists of a series of +1s and -1s.

3. Wilcoxon Signed-Rank Test:

This test procedure is designed to determine whether two matched-pair samples are from the same population. This test is appropriate for "before" and "after" experiments where the same item is measured twice. Accordingly, it can be used to determine whether a specific action leads to a significant change.

4. Spearman Rank Correlation:

This test procedure is used to determine the extent of the relationship between two variables which are measured with rank-order data. The test statistic provides an estimate of the bi-variate correlation coefficient on naturally ranked data and can be interpreted in a similar manner to the Pearson correlation coefficient for quantitative data. The two input data options are:

• **Raw:**

The input consists of the actual measurements for the two variables, which are then rank ordered.

• **Processed:**

The input consists of the ranks for the two variables.

5. Kruskal-Wallis Test:

This test extends the Wilcoxon rank-sum test to more than two groups. The null hypothesis is that the populations of interest are identical.

14.3 DATA INPUT

Problem data can be inputted via terminal prompting or from a data file (see Chapter 2.0). The basic input includes:

◊ Test method

◊ Level of significance (alpha error)

◊ Number of points in Population(s)

◊ Variable values for Population(s)

◊ Data file option

- File name(s)

- Column name(s)

- Column number(s) for variables

Options one through four utilize the standard normal distribution while option five uses the chi-square distribution in computing the critical statistic.

14.4 MODEL OUTPUT

The following highlights the basic output from the nonparametric model:

◊ Sums for each group

◊ Test statistic

◊ Critical lower and upper limit

◊ Conclusion regarding the null hypothesis (i.e., reject or do not reject)

14.5 DEMONSTRATION EXERCISES

EXERCISE #1: Perpetual Savings & Loan is a relatively new lending institution specializing in 1st trust deeds for mid-range housing projects. Perpetual's vice president for mortgage loans is interested in comparing interest rate on 1st trust deeds between the local savings & loan and the local banks. The vice president has collected the following data from a representative sample of 11 S&L's and eight banks:

S&L	BANK
9.50	10.50
9.25	11.00
9.00	9.50
10.25	10.00
10.00	11.00
9.75	10.50
9.50	10.25
10.00	9.75
10.50	
9.75	
10.25	

The vice president would like to know if the interest rates charged by the S&L industry are similar to those charged by the banking industry. The vice president plans to analyze this data using nonparametric methods because of the relatively small sample size and the uncertainty regarding the shape of the populations distributions. More specifically, the vice president wishes to use the Wilcoxon Rank-Sum test at a 0.05 level of significance.

** PROMPTED INPUT **

MODEL OPTIONS

    1. WILCOXON RANK-SUM TEST
    2. RUNS TEST
    3. WILCOXON SIGNED-RANK TEST
    4. RANK CORRELATION
    5. KRUSKAL-WALLIS
       SELECT OPTION (1-5): 1

ALPHA ERROR (0-1): 0.05

NUMBER OF DATA POINTS IN POPULATION #1: 11

NUMBER OF DATA POINTS IN POPULATION #2: 8

NAME FOR VARIABLE #1: ....S&L

NAME FOR VARIABLE #2: ....BANK

	S&L	BANK
1	9.50	10.50
2	9.25	11.00
3	9.00	9.50
4	10.25	10.00
5	10.00	11.00
6	9.75	10.50
7	9.50	10.25
8	10.00	9.75
9	10.50	
10	9.75	
11	10.25	

SAVE DATA (Y/N)?: ....N
SELECT OPTION #7: ....Run Problem

One or Two tailed Test? Enter a '1' or a '2' and press ◄┘ 2

** NONPARAMETRIC MODEL **
RESULTS

		r1	r2
1	=	4	16
2	=	2	18.5
3	=	1	4
4	=	13	10
5	=	10	18.5
6	=	7	16
7	=	4	13
8	=	10	7
9	=	16	
10	=	7	
11	=	13	

TEST METHOD: .... WILCOXON RANK-SUM TEST
ALPHA ERROR: 0.05

POPULATION MEAN:.....................................110

STANDARD DEVIATION: 12.1106

SUM OF GROUP #1:.......................................87

SUM OF GROUP #2:.....................................103

STANDARD ERROR: 23.7368

CRITICAL UPPER LIMIT:...133.7368

CRITICAL LOWER LIMIT: 86.2632

CONCLUSION: ....DO NOT REJECT NULL

These results indicate that there is insufficient evidence to reject the null hypothesis of no difference in interest rates between the S&L's and the banks.

EXERCISE #2: Sam Slooth, vice president of Eye-Spy Investigations Inc., recorded the following number of missing-persons inquiries conducted on 21 consecutive business days. Mr. Slooth wants to determine whether his sample is a random one. Discarding the values which are equal to the median, test for randomness at the 0.01 level of significance.

DAY	INQUIRIES	DAY	INQUIRIES
1	14	11	5
2	5	12	8
3	3	13	12
4	11	14	5
5	9	15	15
6	8	16	17
7	13	17	6
8	15	18	11
9	8	19	9
10	2	20	10
		21	7

** PROMPTED INPUT **

MODEL OPTIONS

    1. WILCOXON RANK-SUM TEST
    2. RUNS TEST
    3. WILCOXON SIGNED-RANK TEST
    4. RANK CORRELATION
    5. KRUSKAL-WALLIS
       SELECT OPTION (1-5): 2

RAW OR PROCESSED (-1s OR +1s) DATA (R/P): ....R

NUMBER OF DATA POINTS IN POPULATION #1: 21

ALPHA ERROR (0-1): 0.01

NAME FOR VARIABLE #1: ....INQ

DAY	INQ	DAY	INQ
1	14	11	5
2	5	12	8
3	3	13	12
4	11	14	5
5	9	15	15
6	8	16	17
7	13	17	6
8	15	18	11
9	8	19	9
10	2	20	10
		21	7

SAVE DATA (Y/N)?: ....Y

** NONPARAMETRIC MODEL **
RESULTS

		r1			r1
1	=	1	12	=	-1
2	=	-1	13	=	1
3	=	-1	14	=	-1
4	=	1	15	=	1
5	=	0	16	=	1
6	=	-1	17	=	-1
7	=	1	18	=	1
8	=	1	19	=	0
9	=	-1	20	=	1
10	=	-1	21	=	-1
11	=	-1			

TEST METHOD: ....RUNS TEST

ALPHA ERROR: 0.01

POPULATION   MEAN:...10.4737

STANDARD DEVIATION:...2.1118

NUMBER OF RUNS:...12

TEST STATISTIC:...0.7227

CRITICAL UPPER LIMIT:...15.9011

CRITICAL LOWER LIMIT:...5.0463

MEDIAN:...9

CONCLUSION: ....DO NOT REJECT NULL

These results indicate that there is insufficient evidence to reject the null hypothesis. Sam Slooth can feel 99% confident that his sample is a random one.

EXERCISE #3: The Director of Human Resources at Allied-Signal needs to measure the impact of sending the company's managers to a human relations course. The director wishes to test the hypothesis that the course will significantly improve the performance of the managers in terms of their interactions with the company's employees. Each participating manager was interviewed by a trained psychologist before and after the course. The resultant pre and post course ranking (1-100 scale) are presented in the following:

Manager	Pre-Course Test Score	Post-Course Test Score
1	29	45
2	35	37
3	28	28
4	38	49
5	36	38
6	42	38
7	38	41
8	37	45
9	52	57
10	48	60

The director plans to analyze this data using nonparametric methods because of the relatively small sample size and the uncertainty regarding the shape of the populations distributions. Because of the matched pairs nature of the data, the director has selected the Wilcoxon Sign Rank test at a 0.05 level of significance.

** PROMPTED INPUT **

MODEL OPTIONS

    1. WILCOXON RANK-SUM TEST
    2. RUNS TEST
    3. WILCOXON SIGNED-RANK TEST
    4. RANK CORRELATION
    5. KRUSKAL-WALLIS
        SELECT OPTION (1-5): 3

NUMBER OF DATA POINTS IN POPULATION: 10
ALPHA ERROR (0-1): 0.05

NAME FOR VARIABLE #1: ....PRE
NAME FOR VARIABLE #2: ....POST

** DATA INPUT **

	PRE	POST
1	29	45
2	35	37
3	28	28
4	38	49
5	36	38
6	42	38
7	38	41
8	37	45
9	52	57
10	48	60

SAVE DATA (Y/N)?: ....N

SELECT OPTION #7: ....Run Problem
One or Two Tailed Test? Enter a '1' or a '2' and press ◄┘............2

** NONPARAMETRIC MODEL **
OUTPUT

TEST METHOD: ....WILCOXON SIGN
ALPHA ERROR: 0.05

		rank	diff
1	=	9	16
2	=	1.5	2
3	=	0	0
4	=	7	11
5	=	1.5	2
6	=	-4	-4
7	=	3	3
8	=	6	8
9	=	5	5
10	=	8	12

POPULATION MEAN:...0

STANDARD DEVIATION:...16.8819

SUM OF SIGNED RANKS:..37

CRITICAL UPPER LIMIT:...33.0886

CRITICAL LOWER LIMIT:..-33.0886

CONCLUSION: ....REJECT NULL

These results suggest that the null hypothesis of no difference can be rejected. That is, the computed test statistic falls outside the critical limits. Accordingly, the director can conclude that the course does seem to improve leadership skills.

EXERCISE #4: The chief executive officer at Rector Transportation Corporation is in the process of evaluating the performance of the company's 10 regional marketing managers. The CEO has collected the following data on leadership ranking (based on a series of psychological tests) and sales ranking (based on sales revenue for the last year) for the ten managers.

Manager	Leadership	Sales
1	2	3
2	4	7
3	7	5
4	9	9
5	6	4
6	3	1
7	8	10
8	1	2
9	5	8
10	10	6

The CEO is interested in determining the extent of the rank order relationship between leadership and sales. The CEO plans to analyze this data using nonparametric methods because of the relatively small sample size and rank nature of the data. The CEO has selected the Spearman Rank Correlation model at a 0.05 level of significance.

** PROMPTED INPUT **

MODEL OPTIONS

1. WILCOXON RANK-SUM TEST
2. RUNS TEST
3. WILCOXON SIGNED-RANK TEST
4. RANK CORRELATION
5. KRUSKAL-WALLIS
   SELECT OPTION (1-5): 4

RAW OR PROCESSED (RANKED)DATA:................................R

NUMBER OF DATA POINTS IN POPULATION #1: 10

ALPHA ERROR (0-1): 0.05

NAME FOR VARIABLE #1: ....LEAD

NAME FOR VARIABLE #2: ....SALE

	LEAD	SALE
1	2	3
2	4	7
3	7	5
4	9	9
5	6	4
6	3	1
7	8	10
8	1	2
9	5	8
10	10	6

SAVE DATA (Y/N) ? ....N

SELECT OPTION #7: ....Run Problem
One or Two Tailed Test? Enter a '1' or a '2' and press ◄┘ 2

** NONPARAMETRIC METHODS **
OUTPUT

TEST METHOD: .... SPEARMAN RANK
ALPHA ERROR: 0.05

		r1	r2
1	=	2	3
2	=	4	7
3	=	7	5
4	=	9	9
5	=	6	4
6	=	3	1
7	=	8	10
8	=	1	2
9	=	5	8
10	=	10	6

POPULATION MEAN:...0

STANDARD DEVIATION:...0.3333

SPEARMAN COEFFICIENT:...0.6848

CRITICAL UPPER LIMIT:...0.6533

CRITICAL LOWER LIMIT:...-0.6533

CONCLUSION: ....REJECT NULL

These results suggest that the null hypothesis of no relationship between leadership skills and sales can be rejected. That is, the computed test statistic falls outside the critical limits. Therefore, the CEO can conclude that leadership skills do influence sales. The computed Spearman r is 0.6848.

EXERCISE #5: The manager of Briggs Department Store is interested in determining the extent of the relationship between monthly sales and the method of payment used by the store's customers. Typically, customers pay for merchandise by one of three methods: cash, store credit or bank credit. The manager has collected the following sales data ($000) by method of payment over the past six months:

Month	Cash	Store Card	Bank Card
Jan	8.5	61.5	64.5
Feb	52.0	57.7	60.0
Mar	44.5	42.0	48.0
Apr	48.0	38.0	41.5
May	50.5	51.0	45.5
Jun	56.0	55.0	52.5

The manager wishes to know if the there is a significant difference in sales by method of payment at the 0.05 level.

** PROMPTED INPUT **

MODEL OPTIONS

    1. WILCOXON RANK-SUM TEST
    2. RUNS TEST
    3. WILCOXON SIGNED-RANK TEST
    4. RANK CORRELATION
    5. KRUSKAL-WALLIS
       SELECT OPTION (1-5): 5

NUMBER OF POPULATIONS: 3

ALPHA ERROR: 1=0.10, 2=0.05, 3=0.025, 4=0.01, 5=Other
       SELECT ALPHA ERROR (1-5): 2

    Degrees of Freedom.............................2
    Critical chi-square 5.99147

NUMBER OF DATA POINTS IN POPULATION #1: 6
NUMBER OF DATA POINTS IN POPULATION #2: 6
NUMBER OF DATA POINTS IN POPULATION #3: 6

NAME FOR VARIABLE #1: X1
NAME FOR VARIABLE #2: X2
NAME FOR VARIABLE #3: X3

	X1	X2	X3
1	58.5	61.5	64.5
2	52.0	57.5	60.0
3	44.5	42.0	48.0
4	48.0	38.0	41.5
5	50.5	51.0	45.5
6	56.0	55.0	52.5

SAVE DATA (Y/N) ? ....N

** NONPARAMETRIC METHODS **

** RESULTS **

	r1	r2	r3
1	15	17	18
2	10	14	16
3	4	3	6.5
4	6.5	1	2
5	8	9	5
6	13	12	11

RESULTS

TEST PROCEDURE: .... KRUSKAL-WALLIS

ALPHA ERROR: 0.05

SUM OF GROUP 1: 56.5

SUM OF GROUP 2: ....56.

SUM OF GROUP 3: 58.5

CRITICAL CHI-SQUARE: 5.9915

KRUSKAL-WALLIS STATISTIC: 0.0205

CONCLUSION: ....DO NOT REJECT NULL

Since the critical chi-square is larger than the computed Kruskal-Wallis statistic, the manager can conclude the sales and the method of payment are not related. That is, monthly sales appear not to be influenced by the payment method used by the customer.

15.0 DECISION ANALYSIS

15.1 PROGRAM DESCRIPTION

This program is designed to solve problems involving both decision making under risk and under uncertainty. If additional information is available in the form of a conditional probability table, the program computes posterior probabilities and the expected payoff of each decision alternative using the revised probability data.

15.2 OVERVIEW

Most business decision problems involve a number of alternatives with various outcomes. In many cases, uncertainty exists about the future consequences of each decision alternative. Traditionally, decision analysis problems can be characterized into one of the following three categories:

◊ **Decision making under CERTAINTY:**   The occurrence of future events is known with certainty.

◊ **Decision making under RISK:**   The occurrence of future events is unknown but can be described through the use of probability data.

◊ **Decision making under UNCERTAINTY:**   The occurrence of future events is unknown and no probability data is available for characterizing the chances of the events.

Clearly, chance and uncertainty play a key role in the last two categories. In both cases, the decision maker must choose the best alternative when the future is uncertain. The standard approach is to define the problem in terms of a payoff table which combines each decision alternative with each possible future state, i.e., state of nature.

One approach for characterizing uncertainty is through the assignment of probabilities to each event, i.e., decision making under risk. The standard approach for analyzing decision making under risk problems is through the use of expected value analysis. Typically, an expected value is computed for each alternative and the decision with the largest expected value is selected. Often the decision maker is interested in knowing the expected payoff under the conditions of perfect information (EPPI). This computation is based on making the optimal decision under each state of nature. The difference between EPPI and the expected value of each decision is the expected value of perfect information. This quantity is the maximum amount that the decision maker should pay for perfect information (EVPI). This value is also equal to the expected opportunity loss associated within each alternative (EOL).

One approach for reducing the level of uncertainty is to acquire additional information on the occurrence of future events. The acquisition of new facts can be used to update or revise the prior probability estimates. However, since most information is not free, the decision maker must weigh the potential benefits of this information with its costs. Furthermore, most information regarding future events is not 100% accurate. Therefore, the decision maker must determine the expected payoff with additional information (EPAI) as a bases for evaluating the worth of the new data. Typically, the new data is presented in the form of a conditional probability table. In most cases, Bayesian analysis is used to revised the prior probability data using the conditional table. If the expected value with additional information (EVAI) is greater than the proposed cost for the information the decision maker should elect to purchase and use the new data.

In some instances, probability data on the occurrence of future events is unknown, i.e., decision making under uncertainty. In these cases, the problem can not be solved using conventional expected value analysis. Instead a subjective approach is used where the decision criterion is dependent on the risk preference of the decision maker. Typically, the following four subjective criterion are used to evaluate problems where objective probability data is unavailable:

◊ **Maximax:** Select the alternative that yields the maximum payoff.

◊ **Maximin:** Select the alternative that yields the maximum payoff from among the minimum payoffs for each option.

◊ **Equal Likelihood:** Select the alternative that yields the largest expected outcome based on the equal occurrence of each state.

◊ **Minimax Regret:** Select the alternative that minimizes the maximum loss.

Generally speaking, the use of each of these criterion can often lead to the selection of different alternatives.

15.3 INPUT DATA

Problem data can be inputted either via terminal prompting or from a data file (see chapter 2). The basic input includes:

◊ Decision making under risk or under uncertainty

◊ Number of decision alternatives

◊ Number of states of nature

◊ Payoff values for each decision state combination

◊ Probabilities for each state of nature (under risk option)

◊ Conditional probability table (optional)

◊ Cost of additional information (optional)

15.4 MODEL OUTPUT

The following highlights the basic output from the decision making under risk option:

◊ Expected monetary values (EMV) for each decision alternative

◊ Expected opportunity loss (EOL) for each decision alternative

◊ Identification of the optimal decision

◊ Expected payoff with perfect information (EPPI)

◊ Expected value of perfect information (EVPI)

◊ Sensitivity analysis of the payoff values (optional)

Additionally, if a conditional table is used the following information is presented:

◊ Revised conditional probabilities

◊ Marginal probabilities

◊ Expected payoff with additional information (EPAI)

◊ Expected value of additional information (EVAI)

◊ A statement whether to purchase the information at the given cost

The decision making under uncertainty option provides payoff analysis for the following criterion: maximax, maximin, equal likelihood and minimax regret.

15.5 DEMONSTRATION EXERCISES

EXERCISE #1: The general partner of Perpetual Investments is interested in formulating an investment portfolio for the next six months. The company has recently raised $500,000 from 20 investors. The general partner has identified the following three investment opportunities: construction company, certification of deposit and precious metals. The major uncertainty affecting this decision involves the future state of interest rates. The general manager estimates that there is a 20% chance that interest rates will increase, a 50% chance that interest rates will remain the same and a 30% chance that interest rates will decrease. The general manager has prepared the following payoff table which shows the net percentage return for each investment as a function of the state of interest rates.

ALTERNATIVE

INTEREST RATES	Construction Company	Certificate of Deposit	Precious Metals
Increasing	-2	6	11
Unchanging	3	6	8
Decreasing	14	6	2

The general manager wishes to know which alternative yields the maximum expected return and what is the impact of changes in the payoffs on the optimal decision.

** PROMPTED INPUT **

RISK(R) or UNCERTAINTY(U): ....R

NUMBER OF DECISION ALTERNATIVES (2-10):......................3

NUMBER OF STATES OF NATURE (2-10): 3

MAXIMIZE OR MINIMIZE (+/-): ....+

ADDITIONAL INFORMATION (Y/N):......................................N

NAMES FOR DECISION ALTERNATIVES:
    ALT #1:...D1
    ALT #2:...D2
    ALT #3:...D3

STATES OF NATURE PROBABILITIES:
    STATE #1:...0.2
    STATE #2:...0.5
    STATE #3:...0.3

SAVE DATA (Y/N)? ....N

NUMBER OF DECISION ALTERNATIVES: 3
NUMBER OF STATES OF NATURE: 3

STATE PROBABILITIES

1 = 0.2
2 = 0.5
3 = 0.3

	D1	D2	D3
S1	-2	6	11
S2	3	6	8
S3	14	6	2

** RESULTS **

CRITERIA	D1	D2	D3
EMV	5.30	6	6.80
EOL	5.10	4.40	3.60
EPPI	10.40	10.40	10.40

OPTIMAL DECISION: .... D3 (#3)

SENSITIVITY ANALYSIS (Y/N)? .... Y

** SENSITIVITY ANALYSIS **

DECISION	LOWER LIMIT	CURRENT VALUE	UPPER LIMIT
D1	NO LIMIT	-2	5.500
	NO LIMIT	3	6.000
	NO LIMIT	14	19.000
D2	NO LIMIT	6	10.000
	NO LIMIT	6	7.600
	NO LIMIT	6	8.667
D3	7	11	NO LIMIT
	6.400	8	NO LIMIT
	-0.667	2	NO LIMIT

These results show that decision D3 (precious metals) yields the largest expected value (6.8%). The expected payoff with perfect information is 10.4%. This suggests that the general manager should be willing to pay a maximum of 3.6% for perfect information on the future of interest rates. The sensitivity analysis presented above shows the range over which the current decision (D3) will remain optimal. For example, D3 will continue to yield the largest expected value as long as the payoff for the combination of construction company and increasing interest rates remains at least 11% (certeris paribus).

EXERCISE #2: The production vice president at Ringwald Printing Corporation is considering the introduction of a new copier system. Three basic alternatives are under investigation: a low speed machine, a medium speed machine and a high speed machine. The major factor influencing this decision is the future demand for copy service. The vice president has estimated that the demand for service during the coming year will either moderate (P=0.3) or good (P=0.7). The vice president has prepared the following payoff table which shows the estimated net return ($000) for the three alternatives. These estimates include the amortization cost of the new copier.

ALTERNATIVES

DEMAND	Low Speed	Medium Speed	High Speed
Moderate	100	50	-100
Good	125	250	325

Before deciding on which machine to purchase, the vice president has decided to obtain an independent estimate on the future demand for copier service. The vice president has received a bid for $25,000 from a local research firm to develop a forecast. Historically, the research firm has predicted moderate demand 90% of the time when demand was actually moderate. Furthermore, the firm has estimated that demand will be good 80% of the time when demand was good. The vice president wishes to know whether to retain the research firm and which machine should the company purchase.

** PROMPTED INPUT **

RISK(R) or UNCERTAINTY(U): ....R

NUMBER OF DECISION ALTERNATIVES (2-10):.....................3

NUMBER OF STATES OF NATURE (2-10): 2

MAXIMIZATION OR MINIMIZATION (+/-):............................+

ADDITIONAL INFORMATION (Y/N):....................................Y

COST OF INFORMATION:..25

NUMBER OF INDICATORS (2-10): 2

NAMES FOR DECISION ALTERNATIVES:
    ALT #1:...D1
    ALT #2:...D2
    ALT #3:...D3

NAMES FOR INDICATOR LABELS:
    INDICATOR #1:..I1
    INDICATOR #2:..I2

STATES OF NATURE PROBABILITIES:
    STATE #1:..0.4
    STATE #2:..0.6

SAVE DATA (Y/N)? ....N

** INFORMATION ENTERED **

NUMBER OF DECISION ALTERNATIVES:............................3
NUMBER OF STATES OF NATURE: 2
COST OF ADDITIONAL INFORMATION:...........................25
NUMBER OF INDICATORS:...........................2

STATE PROBABILITIES
1 =   0.4
2 =   0.6

		D1	D2	D3
1	=	100	50	-100
2	=	125	250	325

		I1	I2
1	=	0.9	0.1
2	=	0.2	0.8

** DECISION ANALYSIS **
RESULTS

DECISION ALTERNATIVES

CRITERIA	D1	D2	D3
EMV	115	170	155
EOL	120	65	80
EPPI	235	235	235

OPTIMAL DECISION:... D2 (#2)

ADDITIONAL INFORMATION ANALYSIS

EPAI:...203

EVAI:...33

COST:...25

CONCLUSION: ....PURCHASE INFORMATION

** REVISED CONDITIONAL TABLE **

	I1	I2
1	0.750	0.077
2	0.250	0.923

** MARGINAL PROBABILITIES **

	I1	I2
1	0.48	0.52

SENSITIVITY ANALYSIS (Y/N)?...Y

** SENSITIVITY ANALYSIS **

DECISION	LOWER LIMIT	CURRENT VALUE	UPPER LIMIT
D1	NO LIMIT	100	237.500
	NO LIMIT	125	216.667
D2	12.5000	50	NO LIMIT
	225	250	NO LIMIT
D3	NO LIMIT	-100	-62.500
	NO LIMIT	325	350

These results show that purchasing the medium speed printer (D2) maximizes the expected return without the use of additional information. The analysis also shows that the vice president should be willing to pay a maximum of $33,000 (EVAI) for the market forecast. Since this amount is greater than the $25,000 price proposed by the research firm $25,000, the vice president should purchase the service and use the forecast.

EXERCISE #3: The chief engineer at Marmax Electronics is considering the construction of a new assembly plant. The two decision alternatives currently under review are to build either a small plant or a large plant. The uncertainty associated with this problem involves the future demand for the output of the plant. In this case, demand can be characterized as either weak, moderate or strong. The following payoff table presents the six possible decision-state combinations where the payoffs represent the net profits associated with each alternative.

ALTERNATIVES
($000)

STATES	Small Plant	Large Plant
Strong	15	35
Moderate	10	18
Weak	8	-5

In this situation the chief engineer must choose between the two alternatives without data on the probability of occurrence for demand.

** PROMPTED INPUT **

RISK(R) or UNCERTAINTY(U): ....U

NUMBER OF DECISION ALTERNATIVES (2-10): 2

NUMBER OF STATES OF NATURE (2-10): 3

NAMES FOR DECISION ALTERNATIVES:
    ALT #1: D1
    ALT #2: D2

** PAYOFF VALUES **

	D1	D2
S1	15	35
S2	10	18
S3	8	-5

SAVE DATA (Y/N)? ....N

** INFORMATION ENTERED **

NUMBER OF DECISION ALTERNATIVES: 2
NUMBER OF STATES OF NATURE: 3

		D1	D2
1	=	15	35
2	=	10	18
3	=	8	-5

** DECISION ANALYSIS **
RESULTS

CRITERIA	DECISION ALTERNATIVES		OPTIMAL DECISION
	D1	D2	
MAXIMAX	15	35	D2
MAXIMIN	8	-5	D1
EQUAL LIKELIHOOD	11	16	D2
MINIMAX REGRET	20	13	D2

These results show that the chief engineer should select option D2 in terms of the first, third and fourth criterion and option D1 in the case of the second criterion.

16.0 STATISTICAL QUALITY CONTROL

16.1 PROGRAM DESCRIPTION

Quality control, an integral component of business, involves a concern to maintain standards of some degree of excellence. Organizations that wish to remain viable in today's increasingly dynamic marketplace must provide reliable products at competitive prices. An effective business plan establishes standards for all operations, including the product or service design phase, the engineering phase, the manufacturing phase, and the delivery phase. Quality can have a strong impact on how the customer chooses among similar products or services provided by competing organizations. Poor quality control can have a strong impact on an organization's efficiency as well as on customer preference. Effective quality control is when suppliers ensure that the product or service that they are providing meets specified quality standards. An organization can maintain high quality standards by implementing systems which monitor reliability and control production or service operations.

Acceptance sampling is a statistical procedure for determining whether a production batch or service level meets specifications. In the case of production situations, the batch may have been produced internally or received from a supplier. Acceptance sampling, as the term implies, means selecting a random sample from the batch to determine if the batch should be accepted or rejected. The Acceptance Sampling Plan model determines the appropriate sample size and level of defective items for specified risk levels.

The Acceptance Sampling Curves model allows exploration of the OC and AOQL curves by direct specification of the lot and sample sizes, and the acceptance number. An operating characteristic (OC) curve shown in Figure 16.1 and an average outgoing quality level (AOQL) curve shown in Figure 16.2 are standard output.

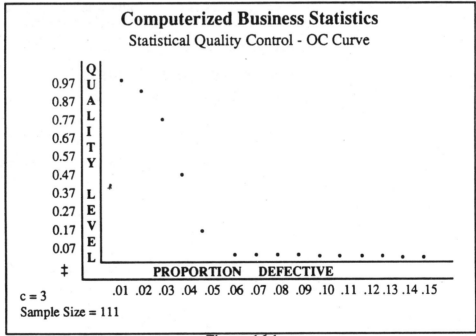

Figure 16.1

121

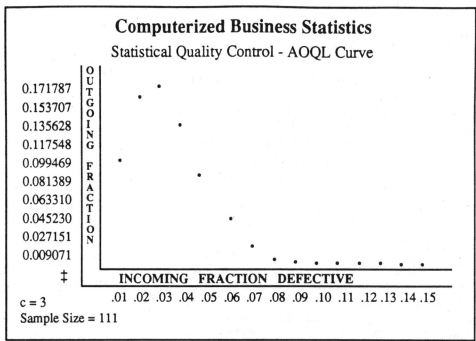

Figure 16.2

Another primary area of concern in maintaining quality involves the actual manufacturing or service process. Several process control methods are useful for monitoring product or service quality. Among the more popular are the C-charts, P-charts, X-bar-charts and R-charts. Your selection of the appropriate control method depends on the specific application and whether the measurements involve attributes or variable values. The Process Control model develops control charts and calculates upper and lower control limits as a means of determining whether the process is in or out of control. Figures 16.3, 16.4 and 16.5 show examples of a P-chart, X-bar-chart, and an R-chart.

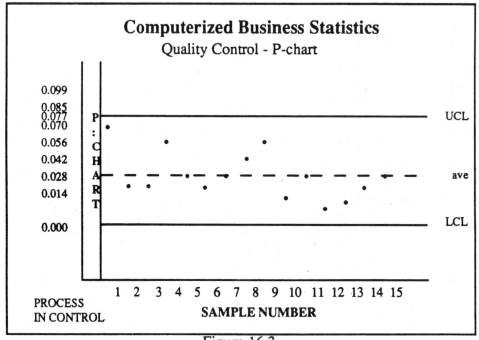

Figure 16.3

122

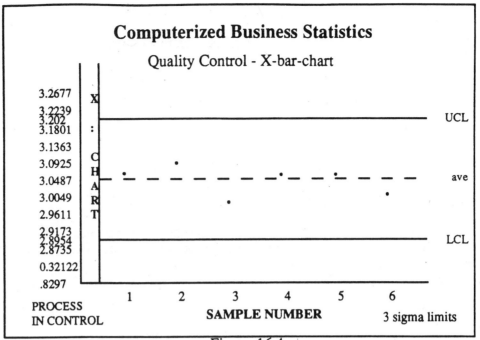

Figure 16.4

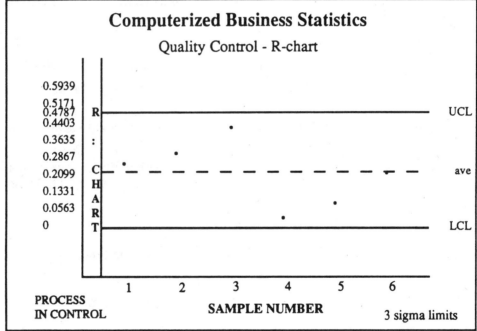

Figure 16.5

16.2 OVERVIEW

The preparation for performing a quality control analysis consists of identifying the desired statistical analysis procedure, collecting the appropriate measurement data, and specifying the error tolerance levels (i.e., Z value).

16.3 DATA INPUT

The first step in the input process is to select the desired modeling approach. The modeling options are:

◊ Process Control

- P-Chart
- C-Chart
- X-Bar-chart and R-Chart

◊ Acceptance Sampling Plan

◊ Acceptance Sampling Curves

The second step in the input process is to enter the prompted data values as listed below. For the P- and C-chart options, the user can specify the appropriate Z value. For the third option, a Z value of 3 is used (i.e., 3-sigma limits).

◊ **Process Control models**

• Number of Samples:	1 to 60
• Sample Size:	• 1 to 5000 for P- and C-charts • 1 to 12 for X-Bar and R-charts

◊ **Acceptance Sampling Plan model**

• Acceptance Quality Level (AQL):	The quality level acceptable to the customer.
• Producer's Risk (Alpha):	The probability of rejecting a lot with a tolerable AQL.
• Lot Tolerance Percent Defective (LTPD):	The lowest quality level acceptable to the customer.
• Consumer's Risk (Beta):	The probability of accepting a lot with a quality level at the LTPD rate or lower.

◊ **Acceptance Sampling Curves model**

• Lot Size (N):	1 to 5000, and must be larger than the sample size.
• Sample Size (n):	1 to 5000, and must be smaller that the lot size.
• Acceptance Level (c):	0 to 10.

The final step in the input process is to specify labels, and to input the data values (process control options).

16.4 MODEL OUTPUT

The primary output for the Process Control models are control charts which include upper and lower control limits (UCL & LCL). The P-chart and C-chart options also include the proportion for each sample. The X-bar- and R-chart options also include the means and ranges for each sample.

The Acceptance Sampling Plan model produces a table showing expected defectives and sample sizes associated with the acceptance levels for the risk levels specified. The acceptance number (c) with the highest LTPD lot size that is smaller than the corresponding AQL lot size is recommended.

16.5 DEMONSTRATION EXERCISES

EXERCISE #1: The audit manager at Greater Pacific National Bank is concerned about the number of complaints associated with the bank's recording of wrong account numbers. She wishes to determine whether the computer encoding of account numbers is within acceptable industry standards or is out of control. She has decided to use a P-chart to evaluate the current system. Fifteen samples were randomly taken from the database at the bank. Each sample contained 100 accounts. The manager wishes to develop 3-sigma control limits.

** INFORMATION ENTERED **

Number of Samples	$1 \leq x \leq 60$	15
Sample Size	$x \geq 1$	100
Z Value	$x \leq 5$	3

	Sam1		Sam1
1	6	8	4
2	2	9	5
3	2	10	1
4	5	11	3
5	3	12	0
6	2	13	1
7	3	14	2
		15	3

** RESULTS **

Upper Control Limit: 0.0762
Calculated Process Average:...0.0273
Lower Control Limit..0

An examination of the resultant control chart (Figure 16.3) indicates that the encoding process is working satisfactorily (i.e., in control).

EXERCISE #2: The manager at Oneonta Product Manufacturing Inc., is interested in tracking the quality of the company's standard three inch marking pen. The manager has decided to collect six samples, each containing four observations. He wishes to develop both an X-bar-chart and an R-chart to determine if the average process and the process variability are under control. The manager plans to use 3-sigma control limits.

** INFORMATION ENTERED **

Number of Samples	$1 \leq x \leq 60$	....	6
Sample Size	$1 \leq x \leq 12$	....	4
Z Value	$x \leq 5$	....	3

Sample Observations

	Sam1	Sam2	Sam3	Sam4
1	3.12	2.95	3.07	3.18
2	3.25	2.98	2.98	3.14
3	2.87	3.04	2.82	3.21
4	3.07	3.06	3.12	3.05
5	3.11	3.01	3.05	3.09
6	3.01	2.89	3.09	3.01

** RESULTS **

Upper Control Limit for X-bar-chart: 3.2021
Calculated Process Average for X-bar-chart:...............................3.0487
Lower Control Limit for X-bar-chart: 2.8954

Upper Control Limit for R-chart: 0.4788
Calculated Process Average for R-chart:...................................0.2100
Lower Control Limit for R-chart: 0.0

Notice that both the X-bar control chart (Figure 16.4) and R-chart (Figure 16.5) indicate that the process is in control (i.e., all of the sample data values fall inside the control limits).

EXERCISE #3: The Director of Quality Assurance at the Wittstone Corporation, is interested in developing a sampling plan for determining whether the latest delivery from the vendor should be accepted. The manager has established an acceptable quality level of two percent, a producer's risk (alpha) of five percent, a lot tolerance of six percent, and a consumer's risk (beta) of eight percent.

** INFORMATION ENTERED **

Acceptable Quality Level (AQL)	$0.001 \leq x \leq 1$ 0.02
Producer's Risk (Alpha)	$0.001 \leq x \leq 1$ 0.05
Lot Tolerance Defective (LTPD)	$0.001 \leq x \leq 1$ 0.06
Consumer's Risk (Beta)	$0.001 \leq x \leq 1$ 0.08

** RESULTS **

	AQL BASED		LTPD BASED	
Acceptance Number	Expected Defectives	Sample Size	Expected Defectives	Sample Size
0	0.0513	3	2.5256	42
1	0.3553	18	4.1682	69
2	0.8176	41	5.6416	94
3	1.3663	68	7.0342	117
4	1.9702	99	8.3767	140
5	2.6130	131	9.6846	161
6	3.2854	164	10.9663	183
7	3.9810	199	12.2280	204
8*	4.6953	235	13.4731	225
9	5.4253	271	14.7051	245
10	6.1689	308	15.9248	265

Acceptance Number (c) = 8   Sample Size (n) = 225

These results show that an acceptance number (c) of 8 and a sample size of 225 provide the desired sampling parameters.

Appendix A: Areas Under the Normal Curve

Example:
If z = 1.96, then
P(0 to z) = 0.4750

z	0.00	0.01	0.02	0.03	0.04	0.05	0.06	0.07	0.08	0.09
0.0	0.0000	0.0040	0.0080	0.0120	0.0160	0.0199	0.0239	0.0279	0.0319	0.0359
0.1	0.0398	0.0438	0.0478	0.0517	0.0557	0.0596	0.0636	0.0675	0.0714	0.0753
0.2	0.0793	0.0832	0.0871	0.0910	0.0948	0.0987	0.1026	0.1064	0.1103	0.1141
0.3	0.1179	0.1217	0.1255	0.1293	0.1331	0.1368	0.1406	0.1443	0.1480	0.1517
0.4	0.1554	0.1591	0.1628	0.1664	0.1700	0.1736	0.1772	0.1808	0.1844	0.1879
0.5	0.1915	0.1950	0.1985	0.2019	0.2054	0.2088	0.2123	0.2157	0.2190	0.2224
0.6	0.2257	0.2291	0.2324	0.2357	0.2389	0.2422	0.2454	0.2486	0.2517	0.2549
0.7	0.2580	0.2611	0.2642	0.2673	0.2704	0.2734	0.2764	0.2794	0.2823	0.2852
0.8	0.2881	0.2910	0.2939	0.2967	0.2995	0.3023	0.3051	0.3078	0.3106	0.3133
0.9	0.3159	0.3186	0.3212	0.3238	0.3264	0.3289	0.3315	0.3340	0.3365	0.3389
1.0	0.3413	0.3438	0.3461	0.3485	0.3508	0.3531	0.3554	0.3577	0.3599	0.3621
1.1	0.3643	0.3665	0.3686	0.3708	0.3729	0.3749	0.3770	0.3790	0.3810	0.3830
1.2	0.3849	0.3869	0.3888	0.3907	0.3925	0.3944	0.3962	0.3980	0.3997	0.4015
1.3	0.4032	0.4049	0.4066	0.4082	0.4099	0.4115	0.4131	0.4147	0.4162	0.4177
1.4	0.4192	0.4207	0.4222	0.4236	0.4251	0.4265	0.4279	0.4292	0.4306	0.4319
1.5	0.4332	0.4345	0.4357	0.4370	0.4382	0.4394	0.4406	0.4418	0.4429	0.4441
1.6	0.4452	0.4463	0.4474	0.4484	0.4495	0.4505	0.4515	0.4525	0.4535	0.4545
1.7	0.4554	0.4564	0.4573	0.4582	0.4591	0.4599	0.4608	0.4616	0.4625	0.4633
1.8	0.4641	0.4649	0.4656	0.4664	0.4671	0.4678	0.4686	0.4693	0.4699	0.4706
1.9	0.4713	0.4719	0.4726	0.4732	0.4738	0.4744	0.4750	0.4756	0.4761	0.4767
2.0	0.4772	0.4778	0.4783	0.4788	0.4793	0.4798	0.4803	0.4808	0.4812	0.4817
2.1	0.4821	0.4826	0.4830	0.4834	0.4838	0.4842	0.4846	0.4850	0.4854	0.4857
2.2	0.4861	0.4864	0.4868	0.4871	0.4875	0.4878	0.4881	0.4884	0.4887	0.4890
2.3	0.4893	0.4896	0.4898	0.4901	0.4904	0.4906	0.4909	0.4911	0.4913	0.4916
2.4	0.4918	0.4920	0.4922	0.4925	0.4927	0.4929	0.4931	0.4932	0.4934	0.4936
2.5	0.4938	0.4940	0.4941	0.4943	0.4945	0.4946	0.4948	0.4949	0.4951	0.4952
2.6	0.4953	0.4955	0.4956	0.4957	0.4959	0.4960	0.4961	0.4962	0.4963	0.4964
2.7	0.4965	0.4966	0.4967	0.4968	0.4969	0.4970	0.4971	0.4972	0.4973	0.4974
2.8	0.4974	0.4975	0.4976	0.4977	0.4977	0.4978	0.4979	0.4979	0.4980	0.4981
2.9	0.4981	0.4982	0.4982	0.4983	0.4984	0.4984	0.4985	0.4985	0.4986	0.4986
3.0	0.4987	0.4987	0.4987	0.4988	0.4988	0.4989	0.4989	0.4989	0.4990	0.4990

Appendix B: Student t Distribution

		Level of significance for one-tailed test				
	.10	.05	.025	.01	.005	.0005
df		Level of significance for two-tailed test				
	.20	.10	.05	.02	.01	.001
1	3.078	6.314	12.706	31.821	63.657	636.619
2	1.886	2.920	4.303	6.965	9.925	31.598
3	1.638	2.353	3.182	4.541	5.841	12.941
4	1.533	2.132	2.776	3.747	4.601	8.610
5	1.476	2.015	2.571	3.365	4.032	6.859
6	1.440	1.943	2.447	3.143	3.707	5.959
7	1.415	1.895	2.365	2.998	3.499	5.405
8	1.397	1.860	2.306	2.896	3.355	5.041
9	1.383	1.833	2.262	2.821	3.250	4.781
10	1.372	1.812	2.228	2.764	3.169	4.587
11	1.363	1.796	2.201	2.718	3.106	4.437
12	1.356	1.782	2.179	2.681	3.055	4.318
13	1.350	1.771	2.160	2.650	3.012	4.221
14	1.345	1.761	2.145	2.624	2.977	4.140
15	1.341	1.753	2.131	2.602	2.947	4.073
16	1.337	1.746	2.120	2.583	2.921	4.015
17	1.333	1.740	2.110	2.567	2.898	3.965
18	1.330	1.734	2.101	2.552	2.878	3.922
19	1.328	1.729	2.093	2.539	2.861	3.883
20	1.325	1.725	2.086	2.528	2.845	3.850
21	1.323	1.721	2.080	2.518	2.831	3.819
22	1.321	1.717	2.074	2.508	2.819	3.792
23	1.319	1.714	2.069	2.500	2.807	3.767
24	1.318	1.711	2.064	2.492	2.797	3.745
25	1.316	1.708	2.060	2.485	2.787	3.725
26	1.315	1.706	2.056	2.479	2.779	3.707
27	1.314	1.703	2.052	2.473	2.771	3.690
28	1.313	1.701	2.048	2.467	2.763	3.674
29	1.311	1.699	2.045	2.462	2.756	3.659
30	1.310	1.697	2.042	2.457	2.750	3.646
40	1.303	1.684	2.021	2.423	2.704	3.551
60	1.296	1.671	2.000	2.390	2.660	3.460
120	1.289	1.658	1.980	2.358	2.617	3.373
∞	1.282	1.645	1.960	2.326	2.576	3.291

Appendix C: Critical Values of Chi-Squared

This table contains the values of χ^2 that correspond to a specific right-tail area and specific numbers of degrees of freedom df.

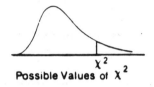

Possible Values of χ^2

DEGREES OF FREEDOM df	RIGHT-TAIL AREA			
	0.10	0.05	0.02	0.01
1	2.706	3.841	5.412	6.635
2	4.605	5.991	7.824	9.210
3	6.251	7.815	9.837	11.345
4	7.779	9.488	11.668	13.277
5	9.236	11.070	13.388	15.086
6	10.645	12.592	15.033	16.812
7	12.017	14.067	16.622	18.475
8	13.362	15.507	18.168	20.090
9	14.684	16.919	19.679	21.666
10	15.987	18.307	21.161	23.209
11	17.275	19.675	22.618	24.725
12	18.549	21.026	24.054	26.217
13	19.812	22.362	25.472	27.688
14	21.064	23.685	26.873	29.141
15	22.307	24.996	28.259	30.578
16	23.542	26.296	29.633	32.000
17	24.769	27.587	30.995	33.409
18	25.989	28.869	32.346	34.805
19	27.204	30.144	33.687	36.191
20	28.412	31.410	35.020	37.566
21	29.615	32.671	36.343	38.932
22	30.813	33.924	37.659	40.289
23	32.007	35.172	38.968	41.638
24	33.196	36.415	40.270	42.980
25	34.382	37.652	41.566	44.314
26	35.563	38.885	42.856	45.642
27	36.741	40.113	44.140	46.963
28	37.916	41.337	45.419	48.278
29	39.087	42.557	46.693	49.588
30	40.256	43.773	47.962	50.892

Appendix D: Critical Values of the F Distribution

Critical Values of the F Distribution at a 1 Percent Level of Significance, $\alpha = 0.01$

Degrees of freedom for numerator

Denominator df	1	2	3	4	5	6	7	8	9	10	12	15	20	24	30	40	60	120	∞
1	4,052	5,000	5,403	5,625	5,764	5,859	5,928	5,982	6,023	6,056	6,106	6,157	6,209	6,235	6,261	6,287	6,313	6,339	6,366
2	98.5	99.0	99.2	99.2	99.3	99.3	99.4	99.4	99.4	99.4	99.4	99.4	99.4	99.5	99.5	99.5	99.5	99.5	99.5
3	34.1	30.8	29.5	28.7	28.2	27.9	27.7	27.5	27.3	27.2	27.1	26.9	26.7	26.6	26.5	26.4	26.3	26.2	26.1
4	21.2	18.0	16.7	16.0	15.5	15.2	15.0	14.8	14.7	14.5	14.4	14.2	14.0	13.9	13.8	13.7	13.7	13.6	13.5
5	16.3	13.3	12.1	11.4	11.0	10.7	10.5	10.3	10.2	10.1	9.89	9.72	9.55	9.47	9.38	9.29	9.20	9.11	9.02
6	13.7	10.9	9.78	9.15	8.75	8.47	8.26	8.10	7.98	7.87	7.72	7.56	7.40	7.31	7.23	7.14	7.06	6.97	6.88
7	12.2	9.55	8.45	7.85	7.46	7.19	6.99	6.84	6.72	6.62	6.47	6.31	6.16	6.07	5.99	5.91	5.82	5.74	5.65
8	11.3	8.65	7.59	7.01	6.63	6.37	6.18	6.03	5.91	5.81	5.67	5.52	5.36	5.28	5.20	5.12	5.03	4.95	4.86
9	10.6	8.02	6.99	6.42	6.06	5.80	5.61	5.47	5.35	5.26	5.11	4.96	4.81	4.73	4.65	4.57	4.48	4.40	4.31
10	10.0	7.56	6.55	5.99	5.64	5.39	5.20	5.06	4.94	4.85	4.71	4.56	4.41	4.33	4.25	4.17	4.08	4.00	3.91
11	9.65	7.21	6.22	5.67	5.32	5.07	4.89	4.74	4.63	4.54	4.46	4.25	4.10	4.02	3.94	3.86	3.78	3.69	3.60
12	9.33	6.93	5.95	5.41	5.06	4.82	4.64	4.50	4.39	4.30	4.16	4.01	3.86	3.78	3.70	3.62	3.54	3.45	3.36
13	9.07	6.70	5.74	5.21	4.86	4.62	4.44	4.30	4.19	4.10	3.96	3.82	3.66	3.59	3.51	3.43	3.34	3.25	3.17
14	8.86	6.51	5.56	5.04	4.70	4.46	4.28	4.14	4.03	3.94	3.80	3.66	3.51	3.43	3.35	3.27	3.18	3.09	3.00
15	8.68	6.36	5.42	4.89	4.56	4.32	4.14	4.00	3.89	3.80	3.67	3.52	3.37	3.29	3.21	3.13	3.05	2.96	2.87
16	8.53	6.23	5.29	4.77	4.44	4.20	4.03	3.89	3.78	3.69	3.55	3.41	3.26	3.18	3.10	3.02	2.93	2.84	2.75
17	8.40	6.11	5.19	4.67	4.34	4.10	3.93	3.79	3.68	3.59	3.46	3.31	3.16	3.08	3.00	2.92	2.83	2.75	2.65
18	8.29	6.01	5.09	4.58	4.25	4.01	3.84	3.71	3.60	3.51	3.37	3.23	3.08	3.00	2.92	2.84	2.75	2.66	2.57
19	8.19	5.93	5.01	4.50	4.17	3.94	3.77	3.63	3.52	3.43	3.30	3.15	3.00	2.92	2.84	2.76	2.67	2.58	2.49
20	8.10	5.85	4.94	4.43	4.10	3.87	3.70	3.56	3.46	3.37	3.23	3.09	2.94	2.86	2.78	2.69	2.61	2.52	2.42
21	8.02	5.78	4.87	4.37	4.04	3.81	3.64	3.51	3.40	3.31	3.17	3.03	2.88	2.80	2.72	2.64	2.55	2.46	2.36
22	7.95	5.72	4.82	4.31	3.99	3.76	3.59	3.45	3.35	3.26	3.12	2.98	2.83	2.75	2.67	2.58	2.50	2.40	2.31
23	7.88	5.66	4.76	4.26	3.94	3.71	3.54	3.41	3.30	3.21	3.07	2.93	2.78	2.70	2.62	2.54	2.45	2.35	2.26
24	7.82	5.61	4.72	4.22	3.90	3.67	3.50	3.36	3.26	3.17	3.03	2.89	2.74	2.66	2.58	2.49	2.40	2.31	2.21
25	7.77	5.57	4.68	4.18	3.86	3.63	3.46	3.32	3.22	3.13	2.99	2.85	2.70	2.62	2.53	2.45	2.36	2.27	2.17
30	7.56	5.39	4.51	4.02	3.70	3.47	3.30	3.17	3.07	2.98	2.84	2.70	2.55	2.47	2.39	2.30	2.21	2.11	2.01
40	7.31	5.18	4.31	3.83	3.51	3.29	3.12	2.99	2.89	2.80	2.66	2.52	2.37	2.29	2.20	2.11	2.02	1.92	1.80
60	7.08	4.98	4.13	3.65	3.34	3.12	2.95	2.82	2.72	2.63	2.50	2.35	2.20	2.12	2.03	1.94	1.84	1.73	1.60
120	6.85	4.79	3.95	3.48	3.17	2.96	2.79	2.66	2.56	2.47	2.34	2.19	2.03	1.95	1.86	1.76	1.66	1.53	1.38
∞	6.63	4.61	3.78	3.32	3.02	2.80	2.64	2.51	2.41	2.32	2.18	2.04	1.88	1.79	1.70	1.59	1.47	1.32	1.00

Degrees of freedom for denominator

131

Appendix E: Critical Values of the F Distribution

Critical Values of the F Distribution at a 5 Percent Level of Significance, $\alpha = 0.05$

Degrees of freedom for numerator

	1	2	3	4	5	6	7	8	9
1	161.4	199.5	215.7	224.6	230.2	234.0	236.8	238.9	240.5
2	18.51	19.00	19.16	19.25	19.30	19.33	19.35	19.37	19.38
3	10.13	9.55	9.28	9.12	9.01	8.94	8.89	8.85	8.81
4	7.71	6.94	6.59	6.39	6.26	6.16	6.09	6.04	6.00
5	6.61	5.79	5.41	5.19	5.05	4.95	4.88	4.82	4.77
6	5.99	5.14	4.76	4.53	4.39	4.28	4.21	4.15	4.10
7	5.59	4.74	4.35	4.12	3.97	3.87	3.79	3.73	3.68
8	5.32	4.46	4.07	3.84	3.69	3.58	3.50	3.44	3.39
9	5.12	4.26	3.86	3.63	3.48	3.37	3.29	3.23	3.18
10	4.96	4.10	3.71	3.48	3.33	3.22	3.14	3.07	3.02
11	4.84	3.98	3.59	3.36	3.20	3.09	3.01	2.95	2.90
12	4.75	3.89	3.49	3.26	3.11	3.00	2.91	2.85	2.80
13	4.67	3.81	3.41	3.18	3.03	2.92	2.83	2.77	2.71
14	4.60	3.74	3.34	3.11	2.96	2.85	2.76	2.70	2.65
15	4.54	3.68	3.29	3.06	2.90	2.79	2.71	2.64	2.59
16	4.49	3.63	3.24	3.01	2.85	2.74	2.66	2.59	2.54
17	4.45	3.59	3.20	2.96	2.81	2.70	2.61	2.55	2.49
18	4.41	3.55	3.16	2.93	2.77	2.66	2.58	2.51	2.46
19	4.38	3.52	3.13	2.90	2.74	2.63	2.54	2.48	2.42
20	4.35	3.49	3.10	2.87	2.71	2.60	2.51	2.45	2.39
21	4.32	3.47	3.07	2.84	2.68	2.57	2.49	2.42	2.37
22	4.30	3.44	3.05	2.82	2.66	2.55	2.46	2.40	2.34
23	4.28	3.42	3.03	2.80	2.64	2.53	2.44	2.37	2.32
24	4.26	3.40	3.01	2.78	2.62	2.51	2.42	2.36	2.30
25	4.24	3.39	2.99	2.76	2.60	2.49	2.40	2.34	2.28
26	4.23	3.37	2.98	2.74	2.59	2.47	2.39	2.32	2.27
27	4.21	3.35	2.96	2.73	2.57	2.46	2.37	2.31	2.25
28	4.20	3.34	2.95	2.71	2.56	2.45	2.36	2.29	2.24
29	4.18	3.33	2.93	2.70	2.55	2.43	2.35	2.28	2.22
30	4.17	3.32	2.92	2.69	2.53	2.42	2.33	2.27	2.21
40	4.08	3.23	2.84	2.61	2.45	2.34	2.25	2.18	2.12
60	4.00	3.15	2.76	2.53	2.37	2.25	2.17	2.10	2.04
120	3.92	3.07	2.68	2.45	2.29	2.17	2.09	2.02	1.96
∞	3.84	3.00	2.60	2.37	2.21	2.10	2.01	1.94	1.88

Degrees of freedom for denominator

Appendix E: Critical Values of the F Distribution

Degrees of freedom for numerator

10	12	15	20	24	30	40	60	120	x
241.9	243.9	245.9	248.0	249.1	250.1	251.1	252.2	253.3	254.3
19.40	19.41	19.43	19.45	19.45	19.46	19.47	19.48	19.49	19.50
8.79	8.74	8.70	8.66	8.64	8.62	8.59	8.57	8.55	8.53
5.96	5.91	5.86	5.80	5.77	5.75	5.72	5.69	5.66	5.63
4.74	4.68	4.62	4.56	4.53	4.50	4.46	4.43	4.40	4.36
4.06	4.00	3.94	3.87	3.84	3.81	3.77	3.74	3.70	3.67
3.64	3.57	3.51	3.41	3.41	3.38	3.34	3.30	3.27	3.23
3.35	3.28	3.22	3.15	3.12	3.08	3.04	3.01	2.97	2.93
3.14	3.07	3.01	2.94	2.90	2.86	2.83	2.79	2.75	2.71
2.98	2.91	2.85	2.77	2.74	2.70	2.66	2.62	2.58	2.54
2.85	2.79	2.72	2.65	2.61	2.57	2.53	2.49	2.45	2.40
2.75	2.69	2.62	2.54	2.51	2.47	2.43	2.38	2.34	2.30
2.67	2.60	2.53	2.46	2.42	2.38	2.34	2.30	2.25	2.21
2.60	2.53	2.46	2.39	2.35	2.31	2.27	2.22	2.18	2.13
2.54	2.48	2.40	2.33	2.29	2.25	2.20	2.16	2.11	2.07
2.49	2.42	2.35	2.28	2.24	2.19	2.15	2.11	2.06	2.01
2.45	2.38	2.31	2.23	2.19	2.15	2.10	2.06	2.01	1.96
2.41	2.34	2.27	2.19	2.15	2.11	2.06	2.02	1.97	1.92
2.38	2.31	2.23	2.16	2.11	2.07	2.03	1.98	1.93	1.88
2.35	2.28	2.20	2.12	2.08	2.04	1.99	1.95	1.90	1.84
2.32	2.25	2.18	2.10	2.05	2.01	1.96	1.92	1.87	1.81
2.30	2.23	2.15	2.07	2.03	1.98	1.94	1.89	1.84	1.78
2.27	2.20	2.13	2.05	2.01	1.96	1.91	1.86	1.81	1.76
2.25	2.18	2.11	2.03	1.98	1.94	1.89	1.84	1.79	1.73
2.24	2.16	2.09	2.01	1.96	1.92	1.87	1.82	1.77	1.71
2.22	2.15	2.07	1.99	1.95	1.90	1.85	1.80	1.75	1.69
2.20	2.13	2.06	1.97	1.93	1.88	1.84	1.79	1.73	1.67
2.19	2.12	2.04	1.96	1.91	1.87	1.82	1.77	1.71	1.65
2.18	2.10	2.03	1.94	1.90	1.85	1.81	1.75	1.70	1.64
2.16	2.09	2.01	1.93	1.89	1.84	1.79	1.74	1.68	1.62
2.08	2.00	1.92	1.84	1.79	1.74	1.69	1.64	1.58	1.51
1.99	1.92	1.84	1.75	1.70	1.65	1.59	1.53	1.47	1.39
1.91	1.83	1.75	1.66	1.61	1.55	1.50	1.43	1.35	1.25
1.83	1.75	1.67	1.57	1.52	1.46	1.39	1.32	1.22	1.00

Appendix F Critical Values of the Studentized Range Distribution (Tukey test)

$\alpha = 0.05$

$n - r$	r 2	3	4	5	6	7	8	9	10	11	12	13	14	15	16	17	18	19	20
1	18.0	27.0	32.8	37.1	40.4	43.1	45.4	47.4	49.1	50.6	52.0	53.2	54.3	55.4	56.3	57.2	58.0	58.8	59.6
2	6.08	8.33	9.80	10.9	11.7	12.4	13.0	13.5	14.0	14.4	14.7	15.1	15.4	15.7	15.9	16.1	16.4	16.6	16.8
3	4.50	5.91	6.82	7.50	8.04	8.48	8.85	9.18	9.46	9.72	9.95	10.2	10.3	10.5	10.7	10.8	11.0	11.1	11.2
4	3.93	5.04	5.76	6.29	6.71	7.05	7.35	7.60	7.83	8.03	8.21	8.37	8.52	8.66	8.79	8.91	9.03	9.13	9.23
5	3.64	4.60	5.22	5.67	6.03	6.33	6.58	6.80	6.99	7.17	7.32	7.47	7.60	7.72	7.83	7.93	8.03	8.12	8.21
6	3.46	4.34	4.90	5.30	5.63	5.90	6.12	6.32	6.49	6.65	6.79	6.92	7.03	7.14	7.24	7.34	7.43	7.51	7.59
7	3.34	4.16	4.68	5.06	5.36	5.61	5.82	6.00	6.16	6.30	6.43	6.55	6.66	6.76	6.85	6.94	7.02	7.10	7.17
8	3.26	4.04	4.53	4.89	5.17	5.40	5.60	5.77	5.92	6.05	6.18	6.29	6.39	6.48	6.57	6.65	6.73	6.80	6.87
9	3.20	3.95	4.41	4.76	5.02	5.24	5.43	5.59	5.74	5.87	5.98	6.09	6.19	6.28	6.36	6.44	6.51	6.58	6.64
10	3.15	3.88	4.33	4.65	4.91	5.12	5.30	5.46	5.60	5.72	5.83	5.93	6.03	6.11	6.19	6.27	6.34	6.40	6.47
11	3.11	3.82	4.26	4.57	4.82	5.03	5.20	5.35	5.49	5.61	5.71	5.81	5.90	5.98	6.06	6.13	6.20	6.27	6.33
12	3.08	3.77	4.20	4.51	4.75	4.95	5.12	5.27	5.39	5.51	5.61	5.71	5.80	5.88	5.95	6.02	6.09	6.15	6.21
13	3.06	3.73	4.15	4.45	4.69	4.88	5.05	5.19	5.32	5.43	5.53	5.63	5.71	5.79	5.86	5.93	5.99	6.05	6.11
14	3.03	3.70	4.11	4.41	4.64	4.83	4.99	5.13	5.25	5.36	5.46	5.55	5.64	5.71	5.79	5.85	5.91	5.97	6.03
15	3.01	3.67	4.08	4.37	4.59	4.78	4.94	5.08	5.20	5.31	5.40	5.49	5.57	5.65	5.72	5.78	5.85	5.90	5.96
16	3.00	3.65	4.05	4.33	4.56	4.74	4.90	5.03	5.15	5.26	5.35	5.44	5.52	5.59	5.66	5.73	5.79	5.84	5.90
17	2.98	3.63	4.02	4.30	4.52	4.70	4.86	4.99	5.11	5.21	5.31	5.39	5.47	5.54	5.61	5.67	5.73	5.79	5.84
18	2.97	3.61	4.00	4.28	4.49	4.67	4.82	4.96	5.07	5.17	5.27	5.35	5.43	5.50	5.57	5.63	5.69	5.74	5.79
19	2.96	3.59	3.98	4.25	4.47	4.65	4.79	4.92	5.04	5.14	5.23	5.31	5.39	5.46	5.53	5.59	5.65	5.70	5.75
20	2.95	3.58	3.96	4.23	4.45	4.62	4.77	4.90	5.01	5.11	5.20	5.28	5.36	5.43	5.49	5.55	5.61	5.66	5.71
24	2.92	3.53	3.90	4.17	4.37	4.54	4.68	4.81	4.92	5.01	5.10	5.18	5.25	5.32	5.38	5.44	5.49	5.55	5.59
30	2.89	3.49	3.85	4.10	4.30	4.46	4.60	4.72	4.82	4.92	5.00	5.08	5.15	5.21	5.27	5.33	5.38	5.43	5.47
40	2.86	3.44	3.79	4.04	4.23	4.39	4.52	4.63	4.73	4.82	4.90	4.98	5.04	5.11	5.16	5.22	5.27	5.31	5.36
60	2.83	3.40	3.74	3.98	4.16	4.31	4.44	4.55	4.65	4.73	4.81	4.88	4.94	5.00	5.06	5.11	5.15	5.20	5.24
120	2.80	3.36	3.68	3.92	4.10	4.24	4.36	4.47	4.56	4.64	4.71	4.78	4.84	4.90	4.95	5.00	5.04	5.09	5.13
∞	2.77	3.31	3.63	3.86	4.03	4.17	4.29	4.39	4.47	4.55	4.62	4.68	4.74	4.80	4.85	4.89	4.93	4.97	5.01

Reprinted by permission of the *Biometrika* Trustees from E. S. Pearson and H. O. Hartley, eds., *Biometrika Tables for Statisticians*, vol. 1, 3rd ed. (Cambridge University Press, 1966).

APPENDIX G

DEVELOPING LOTUS BASED INPUT FILES FOR CBS

The following list outlines the procedure for creating a Lotus based data file for use with CBS. This instruction set assumes that you are in Lotus and that the data base has been created. The Lotus file must be saved using the text file option. The Lotus file must be must contain only numerical values (i.e., no commas or alphanumeric symbols). All CBS input file names must begin with a I-.

1.   Press "/" to display main menu bar if not already shown.

2.   Select "PRINT" from the main menu bar.

3.   Select "FILE" from the print menu bar.

4.   Enter name for the data file (e.g., I-data1)

5.   Select "RANGE" key from menu bar.

6.   Press "HOME" key.

7.   Press ".".

8.   Press "END" key.

9.   Press "HOME" key (All data values should be in the highlighted region).

10.   Press "ENTER".

11.   Select "OPTIONS" from the menu bar.

12.   Select "OTHER" from the menu bar.

13.   Select "UNFORMATTED" from the menu bar.

14.   Select "QUIT" from menu bar.

15.   Select "ALIGN" from menu bar.

16.   Select "GO" from menu bar.

17.   Select "QUIT" from menu bar (Data file is created).